Ronnie James Dio

A Biography of a Heavy Metal Icon

By James Curl

JC Publications
Sacramento, Ca

Ronnie James Dio

A Biography of a Heavy Metal Icon

By James Curl

ISBN 9780692104750

Includes, index, bibliography and chapter notes.
©2018 Copyright by James Curl

No part of this book may be reproduced or transmitted in any form or by any means, graphic, electronic or mechanical, including photocopying, recording, taping or by any information storage retrieval system without the written permission of James Curl.

Cover design by JC Publication
Cover photo by David Plastik

Manufactured in the United States of America

JC Publications
Sacramento, Ca
JC Publication.com
curl88@hotmail.com

Acknowledgments

Writing this book was certainly a labor of love, but I could not have done it without the help of some great people. I would like to thank the following individuals for their contributions: Dick Bottoff, former member of Ronnie and the Red Caps, Mickey Lee Soule, former keyboard player for Elf and founding member of Rainbow, Mike Donohue and Colin Hart, former touring manager for Elf, Deep Purple and Rainbow, Vivian Campbell, former guitarist for Dio, Doug Thaler former member of Elf, Tracy Grijalva, former guitarist for Dio, Jeff Pilson, bass player for Dio, Bob Daisley, former bass player for Rainbow and Dio, Chris Hager, guitarist for Rough Cutt, Rowan Robertson, former guitar player for Dio, Claude Schnell, former keyboard player for Dio, Tommy Rogers, former drummer for the Vegas Kings and Ronnie and the Red Caps, Ralph Miller, Ronnie's childhood friend, Carl Canedy, drummer for the Rods, Joey Cristofanilli, former bass player for Rough Cutt, Sandy Tomes, former managing director at Caribou Ranch, William Padavona, Ronnie's first cousin, Gary Hoey, Martin Popoff, Kory Grow, Joey Belfiore, Dr. Lois Lee, Chas West and Ronnie's cousin David "Rock" Feinstein.

Special thanks to Claude Schnell and Jeff Pilson.

Table of Contents

Acknowledgments.....iii

Foreword.....1

Preface.....4

Chapter 1.   Birth of a Metal God.....6

Chapter 2.   A Real Band.....12

Chapter 3.   The Elf Years.....21

Chapter 4.   Rainbow.....39

Chapter 5.   Black Sabbath.....54

Chapter 6.   Dio.....68

Chapter 7.   Vivian Exits.....87

Photos.   105

Chapter 8.   Dean the Drago.....138

Chapter 9.   Lock up the Wolves and Black Sabbath Once More.....148

Chapter 10.   Dio Once Again.....161

Chapter 11.   Magica Tenacious D and killing the Dragon.....175

Chapter 12.   Master of the Moon.....187

Chapter 13.   Heaven & Hell.....198

Chapter 14.   The Final Curtain.....208

Eulogy.....217

Photos.....218

Discography.....223

Index.....231

Foreword

"It was sometime in the spring of 1993. I was milling around my house frustrated because my sprinklers were leaking and gushing all over the place and, being the least handy human being on the planet, I didn't have a clue what to do. Suddenly the doorbell rings, I go to answer and who is standing at my front door but Vinny Appice and Ronnie Dio. At that time I'd been friends with those guys for about ten years, since Dokken's first tour with Dio at the end of 1983. I'd also been in a band with Vinny (War and Peace) and gotten pretty close to Ronnie as we both shared a love for Indian food."

"Anyway, after welcoming them and a few laughs, I asked them why the honor of the visit. They told me that they were in the process of reforming Dio (Ronnie and Vinny had reunited with Black Sabbath the previous year) and that Jimmy Bain was no longer going to be playing bass with them so did I know of any bass players available? I immediately said yes, ME!!!!!! At that point I had been working with Don Dokken for a year writing and recording much of what was to be the 1995 Dokken album *Dysfunctional*. Mick Brown had recently teamed up with us, but it wasn't looking to be a full-blown Dokken reunion so my feelings were very mixed about it. The instant I thought about being in Dio, I was totally convinced it was the right move to make."

"Nearly every night of Dokken's touring with Dio during the '84 and '85 tour, George Lynch and I would watch the band most every night. They were such a force to be reckoned with, I just knew I had to be a part of it. So, immediately after saying yes, the guys said we should go jam; they had a rehearsal place right down the street. And it really was under two miles from my house to where they were rehearsing. But then I asked of them, does anyone know anything about sprinklers? I already knew Vinny was one of the handiest guys around, and I soon found out Ronnie was pretty good at that as well. No sooner did I mention it before both of them jumped into action. They started running around my yard with a screwdriver and within minutes I had working and efficient sprinklers watering away. Off we headed to go make some music and begin the two-month writing process for one of the most joyous album making experiences of my life with Dio's *Strange Highways*."

"But what that really says about Ronnie (Vinny too—but this is a book about Ronnie!) is all right there. He was undeniably one of the greatest rock voices of all time, but he was also a true friend and never considered himself above anyone or anything. He'd give you the shirt off his back, and gave more to his fans than any other artist I've ever seen or worked with. His work ethic and the degree to which he took music seriously was as deep as any of the great artists of all time, yet he had humor and humility that one almost never sees in an icon of his stature. Incredible musician and bandleader, yet dear friend with a heart as big as an ocean."

"There's hardly a day that goes by since May 16, 2010 (the day he passed away) when I don't think of Ronnie. I still have dreams where he's alive and so many life situations cause me to reflect on him and the many things (and especially laughs) we shared together. And I am by no means the only one who feels and thinks that way. Almost everyone who ever had serious contact with Ronnie has stories like that and feels nearly identical to how I do about our dearly departed friend. He was truly one of a kind and had an amazing gift of connecting with people in such a way that was almost supernatural. He had such a charmed life but he never ever took it for granted or wanted to live off his laurels. Yes, there is so much to miss about Ronnie, but the one consolation, and something that can be shared with the whole world, is the legacy of music that will always be there. Ronnie's life, and the message in a predominance of his songs, was always that of triumph of the human spirit. No person is a slave to the norms and trappings of society. No one has a right to tell anyone what they can or cannot do. Life is there for the taking and he was always there to stand up and shout that out—with the greatest metal voice of all time."

"I am so proud to have worked with Ronnie and to have learned from Ronnie. But I am also so very grateful I could call him a friend. And though I was out of town on the road for his final days, at least my wife and daughter got to be with him to say goodbye in those last precious hours. I arrived back in L.A. moments after he had passed. The plan was to see him at the hospital for what I knew was to be my saying goodbye, but he departed too soon. As a result we had an impromptu gathering at our home with many friends and coworkers of Ronnie's (including Vinny and his brother Carmine) for a tearful yet somehow comforting afternoon of stories and reflection on the life of one of the greatest persons I've ever had the pleasure to know."

"I hope this book and its stories can have the same effect on anyone who reads it, whether they ever had the privilege of meeting the great RJD or not. His is a life of true accomplishment and soulfulness. To this day I can see the smile on his face and the intensity in his eyes as he made his point loud and clear. No one should ever be forced to be the last in line!!!!! RIP Ronnie - we all miss you so much!!!"

Jeff Pilson
November, 2017

Preface

I first became aware of Ronnie James Dio and Black Sabbath in 1982, when I was 12-years-old. There was a graffiti-covered brick wall in my neighborhood that had the words "The Mob Rules" spray painted across it in bold black letters. At the time I only had a vague notion that it was from some band called Black Sabbath. And I certainly had no idea the significance of those words and what part they would play later in my life as my love of music bloomed in my teen years.

Like most kids growing up in the 1980s I played *Dungeons and Dragons* and watched a lot of MTV. I can distinctly remember watching the "Holy Diver" video with Ronnie battling his way through the ruins of a church armed with a great Broadsword and striking down his enemies. The video and song were favorites of mine as well as my friends.

It wasn't until the 1990s that I first witnessed Ronnie in concert. By this time the popularity of heavy metal had fallen considerably, something I still lament to this day. The show was at a small venue in San Francisco, but nevertheless a memorable one for me. The most vivid memory I have of the concert is of course Ronnie's singing. I was only a few feet from the stage so I got a good look at Ronnie. I remember being impressed that such a small person could have such a mighty voice. I was fortunate enough to see Ronnie two more times after that, once in the early 2000s and then on his last tour with Heaven & Hell in 2009.

After Ronnie's passing I waited years for someone to write a book about him. Every so often I would read rumors online about an upcoming biography, but nothing ever surfaced. Having previously written two biographies on former heavyweight champions, I finally got fed up with waiting and said, "To hell with it, I'll do it myself." And so my rock 'n' roll journey began.

I started by reaching out to Ronnie's band mates and family members; some agreed to talk while others refused or never responded. Thankfully, the ones who agreed to chat were willing to share their experiences, stories and love of Ronnie with me.

So, over the course of 16 months and dozens of phone interviews, I finally had Ronnie's story written. At least some of it. I realize that even with the great information and help I had, I could never capture every moment of Ronnie's life and I'm sure I have left out many a great tale. However, my goal for writing this book was to bring out as much of Ronnie's life story as I could. I wanted to show those who are interested what kind of a person he was. I endeavored to be respectful but at the same time while I tried to show his good sides, I wanted to show his flaws as well. I have tried to do this to the best of my ability with the information that was available to me. I sincerely hope in the end I have written a fitting tribute to Ronnie, a man whom I truly respect and believe was a good person. Not to mention the greatest heavy metal singer of all time, period.

James Curl
March 2018

Chapter One
Birth of a Metal God

"I knew I had something when I sang. Unlike learning to play an instrument, it just seemed to be something that was there immediately—a gift."

Ronnie James Dio

The young boy stared up at the stage watching intently as the band plugged in amps, tuned guitars and checked their PA system with a loud, "Check one two! Check one two!" A moment later his attention was drawn to the thunderous pounding of a bass drum. Across the front of it "Rick and the Ricketts" was emblazoned in bold black letters. A few minutes later the lights dimmed low in the auditorium, signaling to the group of kids that the school dance was about to begin. The band opened with one of their most popular tunes, the loud music echoing off walls. As the music played, it moved through the boy's soul and he stood as if he were star-struck, unable to take his eyes off the band. It was then that he thought to himself: *That's what I want to do.*[1] Later that evening he gathered a few of his friends that played instruments and they formed a band; practices were scheduled to start immediately. And from that moment on, inexorable events were set into motion that would help shape the next 50 years of hard rock and heavy metal history.

Ronald James Padavona came into the world with a scream on July 10, 1942 in Portsmouth, New Hampshire. He would be the only child born to Italian-American parents, Patrick and Anna.

Shortly after Ronnie's birth the Padavonas relocated to the small town of Cortland, New York, where

---

[1] VH1, Eddie Trunk interview.

Patrick's parents (Ronnie's grandparents) Anthony and Erminia lived.

Both Anthony and Erminia had emigrated from Italy. Anthony arrived in America in 1910 and Erminia around 1913. The two met in Cortland and were married sometime in 1915 when Anthony was 23 and Erminia was 22.

Like the majority of immigrants, Anthony and Erminia had very limited schooling and could only read, write and speak a little English. With such a limited education, Anthony took a tough, manual labor job at Wickwire Brothers, a wire-drawing mill that produced steel wire, nails and wire mesh products. Anthony would work at the mill for about 40 years, while Erminia remained at home as a housewife. Years later, Ronnie's dad would also work at Wickwire for about ten years, at which time he took a job at SUNY College as a supervisor, overseeing the janitorial department; he would remain at the college until he retired.

During the time Ronnie was growing up, Cortland was a small, middle class community of about 30,000 people with a predominantly Italian population. It was, according to Ronnie, "A great, moral place to grow up."[2]

Growing up in the 1940s and '50s, baseball was just about the most popular sport in America and Ronnie loved sports. It was a passion that would stick with him his entire life. As a kid he played Little League baseball with his childhood friend Nicky Pantas, who would later play guitar in several of Ronnie's early bands. Another boyhood friend, Ralph Miller, played on the Cortland Moose Little League team that was sponsored by the Moose Lodge and American Legion.

"Ronnie was a real nice kid," said Ralph who also played high school ball with Ronnie, "a little shy. We

---

[2] Ibid.

played baseball together. He was pretty good for a little guy."[3]

Ronnie wasn't the only kid on the team that would grow up to be famous. Teammate Gary Wood was drafted out of Cornell University to play quarterback for the New York Giants from 1964-1969.

Like a lot of kids Ronnie dreamed of someday playing professional baseball. His dad however, felt that Ronnie needed a musical education. So at five-years-old, instead of a bat and ball, Ronnie got a trumpet.

"I began playing the trumpet when I was five-years-old," explained Ronnie. "It was baseball I really wanted to play, so I asked my dad if he'd buy me a bat. He said 'No. You need a musical education.' When he got me a trumpet, I said, you can't hit a ball with this thing! I didn't know why I had it. The next day I started music lessons—four hours of practice every day until I was 17."[4]

Playing trumpet would be Ronnie's only formal musical training and turned out to be a good thing. Years later he would say, "I began at five as a trumpet player and applied the same breathing technique to singing."[5]

Ronnie continued, saying, "My outstanding instrument is my voice—thanks to all those years of trumpet practice I learned the breath control that really makes your voice an instrument. My trumpet training was invaluable, from reading music to understanding theory and melody. From the trumpet I learned to sing keeping melody, instead of chords in mind."[6]

Growing up in the Padavona house Ronnie was exposed to a lot of music, particularly opera. The famous American tenor, Mario Lanza was played frequently and had a big influence on Ronnie's singing style. At times

---
[3] Ralph Miller interview with James Curl.
[4] Padavona.com
[5] USA Today, Ronnie James Dio, June 17, 2015.
[6] Padavona.com

Ronnie's dad would sing along and displayed a great voice.

Besides a love of sports and music, Ronnie was a voracious reader. His interests included romance and fantasy novels, such as the works of Sir Walter Scott and the Arthurian legend as well as science fiction. Another great love Ronnie developed as a boy was a fondness for animals, particularly dogs. At around the age of eight he got his first dog, a black Doxen (dachshund) named Cinders that was with him until shortly after graduating high school.

Like most Italian families Ronnie grew up Catholic and went to church every Sunday and attended Sunday school. And like a lot of kids he didn't like to go. Years later he would admit that as a young boy he was frightened by the nuns.

It was in church that Ronnie got his first taste of singing. "I started singing at seven, but I was pressed into it. I was brought up a Catholic, and from an Italian family in a town populated mostly by Italian-Americans, it was normal to be pressed into a creative endeavor. I sang the lead part in a church related function. It's not something I really wanted to do, and not until I was 12-years-old did I really start working at it. I never wanted to sing in a choir. I always disliked being one amongst a greater number. I've always been a very strong-willed person, even at age five, I wanted to do it my way. Luckily, I did it someone else's way for a while."[7]

Growing up in a religious home Ronnie was "raised to be a good kid" and instilled with a stern moral code. He was taught that whenever he was tempted to do something wrong he should ask himself, "Would this make my parents proud?" If the answer was no, he usually wouldn't do it.

By the time Ronnie was in high school he was an accomplished trumpet player and his interest in music

---

[7] Padavona.com

had grown. He was a member of the school's band and orchestra and first chair trumpet player. In addition, he was also the youngest member chosen to play in the school's official dance band and a member of the wrestling team. Tommy Rogers, who became friends with Ronnie while in the orchestra said, "Whenever Ronnie played trumpet and did his solos and a vibrato, he would twitch his nose."[8]

Although Ronnie went through high school as a "little guy" with the nickname "Pygmy," he was extremely popular. Recalling his high school years Ronnie said,

"Yes, I was. I was president of my senior class and was in the National Honor Society. I was always a very good student, and it was always very easy for me. I was very popular. People gravitated towards me. I remember one time the principal called me into his office. I thought, 'Uh-oh, what have I done now?' Because I did a lot of things people didn't know about. I was a real rebellious kid. But he called me in one time and said, 'You know, you have a great responsibility here. When you walk up the street, you have choices. You can go left and you can go right. When you go left, everyone goes left. When you go right, everyone goes right. That's a great responsibility you have there, so make sure you take really good care of it.' And I always remember that. He wrote a letter to my folks, telling them how he thought I was going to be really successful in my life. I guess he saw something that perhaps I didn't. But the responsibility is something that's always stuck with me. Popularity was something that was foisted on me—I was lucky."[9]

During his high school years, when Ronnie began playing in his first band, rock 'n' roll was still in its infancy. Having just been born in the late 1940s, its roots and evolution could be traced back to the 1920s

---

[8] Tommy Rogers interview with James Curl.
[9] Dio: light Beyond the Black, by Martin Popoff, pg16.

stemming from country and blues. Over time and through a cultural meshing of blues, gospel, jazz, western, swing, and country music, rock 'n' roll was formed. Prior to the 1950s before it earned its name "rock 'n' roll," the piano or saxophone was primarily the lead instrument. But that all changed in the mid-1950s when the guitar took center stage.

Early pioneers like Chuck Berry, Goree Carter, and Bill Haley helped make it the dominant instrument as well as developing the classic early guitar sound. By 1957, when Ronnie was getting ready to start his first real band, Elvis Presley, Buddy Holly and Chuck Berry had helped turn rock 'n' roll into a cultural phenomenon.

Excited with the new music coming out, Ronnie and a couple of his friends decided the time was right to get a band going.

Chapter Two
A Real Band

The first "real" band that Ronnie put together was the Vegas Kings in 1957 while still attending Cortland High School. As one would expect, they were a typical 1950s doo-wop/rockabilly band. Although Ronnie would become famous the world over for his powerful vocals, in the Vegas Kings he not only sang, but also played the bass guitar and trumpet. Ronnie's childhood friend Nicky Pantas played lead guitar, while Tommy Rogers, one of Ronnie's high school pals from band, played the drums. A short while later, Jack Musci came aboard to play saxophone.

Recalling the formation of the first band, Tommy said, "There was a band we heard called Bobby Comstock and the Counts, from Ithaca, New York. Ronnie and I heard them and we said, 'Hell we gotta get a band going.' So we got Nicky, who was already playing guitar and started practicing in my parents' cellar for months. I would go down and pick Ronnie up at his house in my 1955 Mercury station wagon, because he didn't have a car. And I would get out of the car and I would hear him blowing his trumpet. I would go into his house and talk to his mom, who was a sweet lady. I would then go upstairs, sit on the bed and keep my mouth shut because Pat was standing right behind Ronnie. Ronnie's got this sheet music on the stand and he's practicing and I can't say a damn word until he's done. Then we would both go to my parents' cellar and practice. So that's where it all started."[10]

As time went by the guys moved their practices into a barn-like garage on Tompkins Street in Cortland that they had converted into a homemade studio. One end was a walled-off booth for the mixers, while the

---

[10] Tommy Rogers interview with James Curl.

remaining section was your basic egg crate-covered walls and ceiling.

The group played at dances almost every weekend and on Sundays they would rent the local American Legion hall, sell tickets, and play in front of the town's kids for two or three hours.

The Vegas Kings didn't last long; they soon changed their name to the edgier Ronnie and the Rumblers. In early 1958 the Rumblers had an opportunity to play their first big show, in Johnson City, New York. There was only one stipulation: the organizer of the show wanted the band to change their name. He felt that the "Rumblers" part was a little too suggestive, and he didn't want any fights to break out at the show. After a quick discussion, the guys came up with the more acceptable Ronnie and the Red Caps. It was a name that would stick around for at least a few years.

Ronnie and the Red Caps were a big hit in Cortland and the surrounding areas. Because of their popularity, they were kept busy playing local dances, and fraternity parties at nearby Cornell University. Over time they were requested to play so many events that the local Musicians Union got upset with the band because the "old timers" couldn't get any gigs.

It was around this time in late 1958 or early 1959 that vocalist Billy De Wolf was added to the band's lineup. His stay however, would be short.

During Billy's stint Jimmy Pantas, Nicky Pantas's older brother and manager of the band, became friends with somebody who owned a private recording studio in Trumansburg, New York. This is where Ronnie and the Red Caps recorded their first and only single on the Reb record label. Billy sings "Lover" on the A-side of the single, and is also credited with writing the song. Side B is an instrumental called "Conquest" written by Nicky and Ronnie. The song showcases Ronnie on trumpet and Jack M. on saxophone. It is unclear how many of these records were pressed but it was certainly under 500, with some sources putting the number at less than 100. The exact recording and release date is lost to history.

Shortly after the release of the single, Billy De Wolf left the band and ended up in prison. This returned the band to its original lineup and allowed Ronnie to take over lead vocals, while still playing bass.

In 1960 Ronnie graduated from Cortland High School and promptly enrolled at the University of Buffalo, with the intention of getting a pharmacy degree. Together with Jack Musci the two began their freshman year while still playing with the Red Caps on the weekend and whenever they could find the time. Jack's father, who wasn't happy that Jack was playing in the band, felt that his son should be concentrating on school. So, he gave him an ultimatum: quit the band or he would quit paying for Jack's college.

By the fall of 1960 Jack had left the band and turned his attention to his studies. He would go on to finish school and become a successful teacher and administrator with the Cortland school system.

With Jack gone, Ronnie decided to bring in Dick Bottoff as a second guitar player. Having gone to see Bottoff play, Ronnie approached him after the show and complimented him on his playing, telling Dick that he was one of the best guitar players that he had ever seen. It was then that Ronnie asked Dick if he would be interested in joining the Red Caps. Such was Ronnie's popularity and status that it was an easy decision for Bottoff; he eagerly accepted.

"I joined the band," said Dick, "after Jack M. and between Ronnie, Nicky and myself we developed a unique 'sound' for our guitars. We were great copy artists with both our instruments and our voices. I sang most of the harmony parts with Ronnie. Nicky and I became close friends during those years. We both were working in a typewriter factory in Groton, New York and playing on the weekends. We became very popular and had to make a decision to go full time and leave our jobs, which we didn't mind doing. It was fraternity heaven back in the early '60s. We would play six jobs on a Cornell homecoming weekend. Some great times for sure!"[11] All told, in an eight-year period, Dick played over a thousand gigs with Ronnie.[12]

In early 1961 the Red Caps went into Riposo Studios to record their second single. This would be the first record on which Ronnie went by the name "Ronnie Dio" and would be the only single released by the Red Caps lineup.

There have been several different stories over the years as to how Ronnie came up with the "Dio" name. Dick Bottoff says that Ronnie got the name from his grandmother and that it's an Italian word meaning God. Mickey Lee Soule claims Ronnie took the name from an infamous Italian gangster named John Dioguardi, who also went by the alias Johnny Dio.

Ronnie claimed, in at least one interview, that he did indeed get the name from the gangster Johnny Dio. "My real surname, Padavona," said Ronnie, "was too long and exotic. It had to be memorable. Wanting to keep my Italian identity, I chose a Mafia boss named Johnny Dio. Not to cash in on his infamy, but because it was short and to the point."[13]

The Red Caps' second single was released on the Seneca label; the A-side played "An Angel is Missing" and the B-side, "What'd I Say." This single is rare with only a small quantity pressed, but not as rare as the Reb single. The exact release and recording dates are unknown. Some sources claim that it came out in 1959, but it probably came out sometime in late 1960. After the single, Ronnie and the Red Caps officially changed their name to Ronnie Dio and the Prophets. The name had been thought up by Ronnie and one of his best friends

---

[11] Padavona.com
[12] Dick Bottoff interview with James Curl.
[13] TeamRock.com, Ronnie James Dio: My life story, September 20, 2016.

Pauli Consroe, during a drive from Cortland to the University of Buffalo in 1960.

Ronnie Dio and the Prophets released a number of singles. The first being "The Ooh-Poo-Pah-Doo" released on January 24, 1962, with "Love Pains" on the flip side. Following the single, the group released their first full-length LP. The album was a live recording done at Domino's restaurant, in Cortland on February 4, 1963 titled: *Dio at Domino's*. The album features some cover songs like "I Left My Heart in San Francisco" and "Great Balls of Fire" by Jerry Lee Lewis, as well as several other famous rock 'n' roll songs. It also contains a number of originals which include "An Angel is Missing," "Follow Me," "Blue Days Blue Nights," and "Make Johnny Blue." The final track on the album is an original called "Love Pains," which came out on the B-side to The Prophets' first single.

"*Dio at Domino's* was indeed recorded at Domino's Restaurant," said Bottoff. "And believe me, I know our music still echoes in the rafters."[14]

Following the *Dio at Domino's* LP, the band released several singles starting in 1963. The first was "Swingin' Street," released in August, backed with "Gonna Make It Alone." After that came the one-sided single of "Will You Still Love Me Tomorrow" followed by "Mr. Misery" and "Our Year" released in November. The group then did a version of the rock 'n' roll classic "Love Potion Number Nine," released in January 1964. This single had the same song on both sides, so radio stations wouldn't play the wrong side.

In 1964, after recording "Swingin' Street," a New York promoter named Simon Breme decided that the single should be promoted by sending Ronnie on tour with Bobby Comstock's band. In the meantime, Nicky, Tommy and Dick, along with bass player Joe Leo, would

---

[14] Padavona.com

head over to Sweden for ten weeks to push the single and be the warm-up act for international star Lil Babs.

"Sweden really was nuts over her and us too," said Bottoff. "We were the opening act for her and I sang 'Swingin' Street' as Ronnie."[15]

It was around this time that Ronnie married his girlfriend Loretta Berardi at St. Anthony's Catholic Church. Like Ronnie, Loretta had grown up in Cortland. Their marriage, however, was doomed from the start. Being a small town girl, Loretta didn't like Ronnie playing in a band or his rock 'n' roll lifestyle.

"Nicky and I would pull up with the van outside Ronnie's house," said Dick, "and we would have to wait there 20 or 30 minutes. He knew we were there. And inside Loretta was telling Ronnie not to go and that he was better than this. We never knew about it at the time; we found out about it later. That's actually one of the reasons they split—he just couldn't take that kinda talk from her any longer."[16]

Doug Thaler arrived in Cortland in September of 1963 to attend SUNY State University. Having played in bands for several years as a guitarist and keyboard player he was anxious to find out what the local music scene was like. A few days after moving into town Doug attended a local "mixer" where Clay Fulton and the Cindells were playing. After watching the band, he thought that they were one of the best live acts he had ever seen. Doug would eventually acquaint himself with the band and become friends with the members, one of whom was a local boy named Dave Feinstein, who played drums and was all of 15-years-old.

It didn't take long for Doug to learn that the music scene in Cortland was hot. There were a lot of bands and

---
[15] Ibid.
[16] Dick Bottoff interview with James Curl.

because of the numerous colleges in the surrounding area there was always a gig available for a decent group. It also helped that the drinking age in Cortland was 18 at the time and the bars were always packed and looking for entertainment.

During the fall of 1963 Doug had joined a band called The Legends and began asking around who the best singer in the area was. Without hesitation, everyone he talked to would say, "Ronnie Dio, the singer for Ronnie Dio and the Prophets." Doug learned that the band had a few singles out and had gotten some airplay on the local Cortland and Syracuse radio stations.

Interested, Doug went to see the band play, which at the time had the lineup of Ronnie, Dick Bottoff, Nicky Pantas and Tommy Rogers. "The Prophets were doing the typical music of the day," said Doug, "like 'Portrait of My Love,' 'Jezebel' and 'I Left My Heart in San Francisco.' Seeing them for the first time, I thought that they were really good."[17]

By 1965 Doug had been accepted into the local music scene with his band The Legends. It was at this point that he met Ronnie for the first time in April when The Legends played Little York Park in Cortland on a beautiful spring day. Following a short conversation the two became acquainted.

By the fall of '65 The Legends had broken up and Doug had joined Brian's Idols, one of the better bands in the area. Doug and Nicky had also become great friends. Nicky, who was technically savvy, had a tape recorder in his front bedroom on which he and Doug would record original songs. Nicky would then engineer them down in his homemade studio that he had set up in the basement.

"Nicky was a great guitar player in the context of that day," said Doug. "He could play anything that anybody put into rock records of those days. He also produced most, if not all, of the recordings those early bands made.

---

[17] Dough Thaler interview with James Curl.

He was way ahead of his time with respect to mastering the use of the recording equipment available in those days. I remember a version of 'Will You Still Love Me Tomorrow' that The Prophets did in 1963. It was never released but it was amazing. Nicky had figured out a way to record only the echo from his guitar and not the original signal. He made it sound like a string section—you could not tell the difference."[18]

Back in 1964 Tommy Rogers had left The Prophets and was replaced for a short time by Jack Shelton. Jack was in turn replaced by Gary Driscoll when Jack went into the Navy. A year-and-a-half later, in the fall of 1966, Dick Bottoff decided to leave the band. "I actually left the band," said Dick, "because I had an opportunity to learn about computers and at that time Ronnie was beginning to lose interest. I'm not exactly sure why but Nicky and I had to almost drag him from his house to play the jobs. I thought it might be time for me to change careers. I don't regret leaving but I think I might have in some ways woke Ronnie up to the fact that his career was stalled and he'd better get motivated."[19]

To replace Dick, Ronnie recruited his younger cousin Dave Feinstein to play rhythm guitar. To get Dave up to speed, Dick and Doug worked with the young guitarist. "I lived around the corner from David's parents' house," said Doug, "and I remember teaching him the chords to some of the covers The Prophets were playing in those days."

By 1967 Doug was regularly playing and writing with the members of The Prophets. Together with Nicky and Dave the three had recorded a demo called "Hey, Look Me Over." The song featured Doug on vocals and guitar, Nicky on bass and Dave on the drums. The demo got into Ronnie's hands and after listening to it he was immediately excited. He invited Doug, along with the

---

[18] Padavona.com, Doug Thaler.
[19] Ibid.

rest of the band to go to New York where they recorded the song with Doug singing, as well as another Ronnie and Nicky had composed together. "Hey, Look Me Over" and "It Pays to Advertise" were recorded in New York City in July of 1967, with the lineup of Ronnie, Dave, Nicky, Gary and Doug.

Following the recordings, The Prophets were offered a spot as a supporting act for the popular Gene Pitney, who had a number of Top 40 hits. At the time, Nicky was suffering from a bad ulcer and was unable to travel and do the required lifting of heavy amps and equipment. He suggested that Ronnie take Doug in his place while he seek medical treatment.

Throughout July, August and September Doug played on the road with The Prophets as Pitney's opening act. As a result of his doing so, he was tossed out of Brian's Idols and added to The Prophet's roster as long as he agreed to play piano. "I agreed to play piano, which I did, but not very well," said Doug. "I saw my job as mainly to be the primary harmony singer and songwriter."[20]

With Doug in the band and a new single on the way everyone was excited and things were about to start changing for Ronnie Dio and his Prophets.

---

[20] Dough Thaler interview with James Curl.

Chapter Three
The Elf Years

By the mid-1960s the rock 'n' roll scene had begun to change. The doo wop bands of the 1950s and early '60s were giving way to a fresh new high energy rock 'n' roll that was indicative of the changing musical and cultural landscape. Crew cuts, pompadours and duck tails were going out of style. Hair was getting longer, guitars, once held high and neat, were starting to slump low and were getting louder and more distorted. Vocals and lyrics, once reserved, were becoming bolder and edgier.

In the United States bands like the Doors, Jimi Hendrix, and the Byrds were helping usher in a new psychedelic era of rock. While across the pond, Deep Purple, Led Zeppelin and Black Sabbath were creating a heavier sound that was a precursor of things to come. For Ronnie and his band mates these developments couldn't have come along at a better time.

Adapting to the changing times, The Prophets began to morph. They traded in their clean-cut appearance and pressed suits for denim jeans and long hair. And the first manifestation of Elf, known initially as the Electric Elves, was born in mid-1967. It would be this band that really put Ronnie on the path of heavy metal destiny.

The name was a direct reflection, and a joke pertaining to the elf-like height of the band's members: Ronnie at 5'4", Nicky at 5'3", and Dave Feinstein at 5'1".

"Nicky used to wear Beatle boots," said Doug, "and, with the weather being what it is in Cortland, his shoes got wet a lot. The toes of his Beatle boots curled up and made him look like an elf. I started hanging out with him a lot by my senior year of college (1966) and I actually called him 'Elf' instead of Nicky, or his regular nickname of years, 'Gump.' I used to refer to them as 'the Electric Elves' as a joke but they actually decided to use the name on the 'Hey, Look Me Over' release."

"In the fall of 1967, we had bookings under both names. In places where Ronnie Dio and the Prophets had played repeatedly we still used that name. For all new bookings into new areas, we were the Electric Elves."

It was around this time that Ronnie began going by the name he would become synonymous with for the rest of his life: "Ronnie James Dio."

The Electric Elves toured extensively starting in late 1967, playing many of the same places that Ronnie Dio and the Prophets had played. Ronnie was still handling both vocals and bass, while Nicky and Dave respectively shared the guitar duties. Gary Driscoll kept the beat, and Doug played the keyboards and piano. After the shows the band would hang out at the venues to mingle with fans, shoot darts, drink beer and smoke cigarettes.

In October, their first single which included the songs "Hey, Look Me Over" and "It Pays to Advertise," was released under the Electric Elves moniker. Two months later, on February 12, 1968 tragedy struck. While driving back from a gig late at night in Waterbury, Connecticut along Route 8, Ronnie's van was hit head on by a drunk driver. "We started up Route 8," said Thaler. "It was very snowy, the snow banks were stacked high and we were in Ronnie's van. We had just crossed into Massachusetts. A guy was coming the other way pretty fast and headed right for us. No matter what Nicky did he could not avoid the guy and finally it was a head-on collision at 55 mph."[21]

Nicky, who was driving, was crushed by the steering wheel and killed. Ronnie, riding in the passenger seat, went through the windshield and ended up on the street. It would take over 150 stitches to put his scalp back together. His cousin Dave suffered a broken ankle and facial lacerations that required dozens of stitches. Doug had his left thigh crushed. The injury was so severe that he very nearly had to have his leg amputated. He ended

---

[21] Doug Thaler interview with James Curl.

up in traction for weeks to align the bone fragments and then a body cast for three months. In addition, he also suffered nerve damage to his left arm. Gary was lucky and escaped relatively unscathed with only a few bumps and bruises.

"I was in the back seat," said Dave Feinstein. "I don't remember the accident 'cause I was in shock. I didn't realize it until I woke up in the hospital. I had a big cut in my lip and a big cut under my eye and a broken ankle. The whole van was destroyed and our equipment was trashed. I woke up in the hospital in the same room as Ronnie and he was in the next bed over. And we just looked at each other and we looked like monsters because we were all swollen up. Basically, Ronnie had his whole scalp torn back and he had over a hundred stitches. Then we found out that Nicky got killed—it was a traumatic experience."[22]

Dick Bottoff recalled the accident saying, "Jimmy Pantas called me at 1:30 in the morning to tell me that Nicky was dead. The whole town was devastated."[23]

A few weeks after the tragic accident, and while Doug was still healing, Ronnie, Dave and Gary reassembled what was left of the band. In May of 1968, to replace the still healing Doug, Mickey Lee Soule was brought in to play keyboards. Mickey, who had been playing piano since he was six, eventually started playing in bands as a teenager. He had grown up in Cortland and knew Ronnie through their shared music connections. At the time, Mickey was playing in his own band called Mickey and the Persians.

"Ronnie was a few years ahead of me in school," said Mickey, "and had the first rock 'n' roll band in town. When I was 13 or 14-years-old he was my idol. By this time, I'd been playing for a while and was friends with everyone in the group. When the band reformed, I got a

---

[22] Dave Feinstein interview with James Curl.
[23] Dick Bottoff interview with James Curl, November 19, 2016.

call from Ronnie and he asked if I wanted to be in the band, and I said yes, as quickly as I could say it. We began rehearsals in a basement. I can't imagine what we must have looked like. Ronnie still had half of his head shaved and a big scar from the wreck, and Dave still had a cast on his ankle."[24]

For about three months the band performed as a four-piece with Ronnie, Gary, Dave, and Mickey Lee. Together, they traveled all over the eastern portion the United States. During one particular outing the band had gotten done playing a show and returned to their motel rooms. A short while later Ronnie and Mickey Lee headed out to find a restaurant where they could get some takeout. After driving all over town they finally found a little diner that was basically a roadside truck stop.

Ronnie and Mickey made their way into the place and right away they realized that they didn't fit in. With their hippie look and long hair the customers eyed them with disdain. "We went in," said Mickey Lee, "and of course we had the long hair and everything and this was back in the day when long hair was just starting become the thing among the young, but not so much the truck drivers."

Brushing off the looks, Ronnie and Mickey proceeded to the front counter and placed an order. A moment later a fork came flying across the room and landed on the floor next to Ronnie's foot. The first thing Mickey Lee thought was, *Oh no, here we go.* "But to my utter surprise and shock," said Mickey, "Ronnie turned around and says loudly, 'Who threw that fucking fork! Did somebody throw that fork at me?'" Mickey, too shocked to say anything, just stood there speechless, thinking to himself, *What are you doing? The place is packed with huge truck drivers.*

To Mickey's astonishment, nobody said a word and the place went completely quiet. Ronnie and Mickey

---

[24] Mickey Lee Soule interview with James Curl, November 28, 2016.

then paid for their meal and left the diner. As they exited the place they became anxious and walked quickly to their car. Hastily they jumped in and sped off down the highway. "That was Ronnie," said Mickey. "He wasn't about to take any shit from anybody."[25]

Several months later in August of 1968 Doug was finally freed of his body cast. Rejoining the band, he technically replaced Nicky as lead guitarist. Unfortunately, because of the accident, Doug had suffered nerve damage to his left arm that affected his playing, while Dave's guitar playing had vastly improved. As a result, Dave eventually took over most of the lead guitar work.

By the end of 1968 the band had decided to change their name with the hopes of creating a new image. "We just dropped the 'Electric,'" said Doug. "It had already become dated and we just quit using it."[26] And thus, the Elves were born.

The name change occurred just a few months before their second single on Decca Records was released. The single was recorded at Columbia's 30th Street studio (called The Church) on Thanksgiving Day of 1968, and included the songs "Walking in Different Circles," backed by, "She's Not the Same." In July or August of 1969 the Elves released another single with the songs "Amber Velvet" and "West Virginia."

It was around this time that Ronnie and Loretta adopted a baby boy named Danny. The decision to adopt a child may not have been the wisest choice. Ronnie and Loretta were still having persistent disagreements about Ronnie's pursuit of a musical career. As a result, by the early 1970s, when Ronnie's career started to take off, the two divorced. Loretta stayed in Cortland and raised Danny, while Ronnie went in pursuit of rock 'n' roll

---

[25] Ibid.
[26] Padavona.com

stardom. Ronnie and Dan would see each other sporadically over the years and stay in touch throughout Ronnie's life. At times, when Ronnie came through town on tour he would invite his son to the shows or occasionally fly him out to California for a visit. Years later, when he was all grown up, Dan would become a gifted writer and horror novelist.

The Elves stayed intact with the current lineup until January of 1972. At that point, Doug decided to quit. He felt that they had gone as far as they could, and that they could not compete with the big names in the business such as Pete Townsend and Joe Walsh. The band had been passed up by several record companies and Doug was getting discouraged. "I thought, I better find something else to do with my time," said Doug. After leaving, Doug would remain involved in the music industry and eventually become the manager of the notorious band Mötley Crüe.

After Doug's exit, Ronnie and the boys once again decided that a name change was necessary. After some discussion, they agreed to shorten the band's name further by simply calling it Elf.

With Doug gone, Dave took over the lead guitarist responsibilities full time. The newly named band continued to play and earn a living by touring across the eastern part of America while actively look for a recording deal. Fans who witnessed Elf remember them fondly.

"It's burned in my visual memory," said one Elf fan named Tony D., "as well as my audio memory forever. I'm 50 now, but for all intents and purposes, I'm still 17 or 18, and at either the Lower Level or St. Joseph Auditorium, in Hazleton, Pennsylvania. It's a Sunday night in the summer, and the sight of would-be hippie chicks in their tube tops or t-shirts with no bra and hard nipples, and low-slung bellbottom jeans with bare midriff was more than I could take. Some were barefoot, 'de rigueur' for the day. A crowd, a huge crowd, always gathered outside the venue, wherever it was, waiting for the band, and they were like nothing we had ever seen before in this small coal mining town of 29,000."

"The huge silver truck parked outside, and the muffled sounds of a roadie inside saying, 'check, one, two... check one, two' indicated that the doors would soon open, and when they did, there was a rush inside after paying the $2.50 cover charge. Imagine that, $2.50 to get in."

"All of us 'would-be's,' meaning simply that as a 'would-be' you fell into two categories: (A) You wanted to be in a band, but your parents wouldn't buy you a guitar when you were in your teens and music started to excite your loins, or (B) You did play in a band (local, of course), and only dreamed of what you could/would be. Well, we all would rush to surround the band as they tuned and got ready to start; they barely had any breathing room. The crowd got so close, and we barely had eardrums left. The Elves were, quite simply, the most professional band to ever play in the town, at the time. We had never seen anything quite like them before. Incredibly long hair, mid-back and thick, all one length on all of them. Stacks of equipment like we had never seen before and could only hope to have. Marshall amps and Sunn PA system, stacked so high you'd swear the roadies had to put on spike boots and breathing apparatus to climb them to disassemble when they were done for the night."

"The band did a combination of cover tunes from the prominent albums of the time, as well as a few cuts from their own. Lots of Led Zep, The Who (*Tommy*, in entirety), *Abbey Road*."

"Ronnie Dio was, of course, always the main front man, and occasionally, Doug would be featured. In our case, as would-be virtuosos, we would not take our eyes off of Dave Feinstein, our idol, who at, what? 5'1" might as well as been the Jolly Green Giant the way he handled that sunburst Gibson guitar with deadly accuracy, especially during the Led Zeppelin covers. Me? I used to watch Mickey Lee Soule, since I was an aspiring keyboardist and could only hope that I could save enough money to buy a Fender Rhodes like his. And I might add that as time went on, I noticed that he changed to an electric piano that had no moniker on it, don't know what it was. As a matter of fact, I also recall seeing him use a small 'miked' upright one or two times, and if I recall correctly, it was a true honky tonk, and after their first alum was out, in which case, since his parts/solos were so 'Leon Russell-esque,' it made sense."

"I remember that Davey had a 'very close female friend' whom he saw every time they played the area. She was as tiny as him, and although I do remember her name, I'll keep it anonymous and tell you that she now lives in the Caribbean, happily married with kids."

"Ronnie never relinquished his bass for a mic—he was the bass player, period, and of course, as his career grew over the years and his prominent voice took center stage with other bands that changed. My friend, who was a drummer, used to talk to Gary Driscoll during the band's breaks, so, of course, being the starry-eyed guy that I was, I joined in. We would ask him question after question about his equipment, the band's equipment, etc. Gary was a very quiet guy, and I remember now, thinking back, that he looked like a young Beau Bridges (the actor), facially, except of course for the super-long hair."

"The Elves played Hazleton, I think, probably 50 times in several years. Always drew a crowd. Hell, I could remember a blizzard and these guys still made it to Hazleton from New York, and the place was still packed!"

"Every once in a while, they would play with other bands from the Cortland and Binghamton area, like Free Will and Brian's Idols, who were also very, very good, but no match for the Elves, not only in their 'polish,' but in their presence too. I think the only other band that came close to them was Wool (formerly Ed Wool and the Nomads). There was always an argument, who was better, and Ed Wool did indeed play a mean geetar that could go one-on-one with Davey Feinstein, but somehow Davey just had a presence to him that made him the favorite among all the aspiring guitarists."

"In their own way, and this is an observation, the Elves actually helped the other New York bands that came down to play, most of them from either Cortland, Binghamton, or Watertown. Once word got around that there was a gig at either the Lower Level or St. Joe's Auditorium, and that the band was from New York, we just presumed that they were as good as the Elves. Somehow, they never were. Somehow, we were always disappointed, but because of our presumption, there would be a crowd for the night and I'm sure that premise followed through at other venues and other areas as well."[27]

Another fan, Mike Donohue, vividly recalls seeing the Elves and Elf on more than one occasion. "It was the fall of 1969 in Auburn, a small town located about 25 miles from Cortland, New York, where Ronnie James Dio was raised and came to prominence. I had just started high school, and had, at that point, seen a total of two bands perform live: the first at my eighth grade graduation dance, the second an outdoor show over the summer, both by local bands. The novelty of hearing a 'real' group perform live before our very eyes, rather than seeing them lip-synch on television had not worn off."

"My friends and I were quite excited about an upcoming dance at Mt. Carmel, the Catholic high school across town, as we had heard that one of the members of this group the Elves had actually made some records,

---

[27] Padavona.com, Tony D.

which was true stardom in our youthful eyes. We couldn't wait."

"The evening arrived, and we paid our $1.25 to get in. Entering the darkened gymnasium, we were met by a sound both exciting and slightly frightening: an unbelievably loud, but clean, hiss from the stage, which we recognized after a moment as idling amplifiers... *lots* of them, with multiple pilot lights glowing in the dark. Budding musician wannabes that my friends and I were, we had all gone stag to check out the band, and huddled up to the stage to take in the gear before the Elves took the stage."

"The biggest amps we had seen to date were small by even local standards. We were agog at what we saw. A veritable wall of amplifiers, more on that one stage than the entire inventory of any music store we had been in to date. Stage right, two full Marshall stacks, with a Y-cord going into both heads for one of the guitarists, whom we would learn was David 'Rock' Feinstein, Ronnie's cousin, and later founder of The Rods. We recognized the bass rig, which Ronnie was to play through, as dual Sunn cabinets, on their sides and stacked on top of each other with the head atop. Our initial impression of the microphone stands was thought to be a joke; they were set so low that we thought it must be a pun on the band's name, and that obviously when the musicians came out they would raise them to their proper height. Not so, as we discovered when they came out that Ronnie himself was 5′2″ and David topped out at an even 5′0″."

"The large fluorescent gym lights abruptly went off, causing a squeal of delight from the crowd that lasted only a second when suddenly there was an absolute explosion of sound and light from the stage. Explosion is an over-used term, but not that night. It was literal, and it was real. Nothing prepared our barely-adolescent minds for what unfolded. The band: Dave Feinstein–guitar, Doug Thaler–guitar and vocals, Mickey Lee Soule–piano and backing vocals, Gary Driscoll–drums, and Ronnie Dio (he hadn't started using the 'James' yet) on bass and lead vocals, played louder than we thought volume actually went. It was unbelievable, yet immediately apparent that it wasn't just the number of amplifiers used, but the power and command of the playing of the instruments that really gave this band its force."

"Ronnie could not honestly be called the 'star' of this band. Not yet. They were truly a group of five equals, all extraordinarily proficient on their instruments and in their songwriting, as the few tunes that they announced as 'one of our own' showed. Ronnie did three quarters of the lead vocals, Doug the others. Ronnie, however, quickly showed extraordinary depth and breadth in what he was capable of singing. The powerful growl and gravel in his voice that is so well known and loved by those of us who are fans of his later work was matched by a smooth, sheer beauty on the more tender numbers."

"We were stunned when the band came out for their second set and Ronnie said, 'Some people wanted to hear something from *Abbey Road*, so we're going to do the whole thing.' The album hadn't been out that long. We were amazed that a band could learn that complex a piece so quickly, and how Ronnie was able to effortlessly nail the sweetness of 'Sun King' or 'Something,' and when Doug, Mickey and Ronnie joined together on 'Because' it was truly one of the most beautiful things I had ever heard."

"We were lucky to grow up where and when we did. I saw the Elves play at our high school dances about ten times between that first show in the fall of 1969 and spring of 1973 when I graduated. The final time I saw the band was shortly after Doug Thaler left, an evening in which I got to meet Ronnie face to face for the first and only time."

"There are many recordings of Ronnie's early years with Ronnie and the Red Caps, Ronnie Dio and the Prophets, the Electric Elves, and the Elves which I have hunted down through the years. It was by hunting down and listening to his earliest recordings that I got an appreciation for the career development that had led to the performer I saw throughout my four years of high school. There is an extraordinary amount of officially unreleased material, live and studio, which stands as a great legacy to Ronnie the performer. Some of it, thankfully, saw the light of day a couple of years ago when the 'And Before Elf... There Were Elves' CD was released."

"Imagine how thrilled I was to open up the sleeve and discover a photo that I had taken inside: Mickey Lee playing the piano, which was taken at the first performance in Auburn after the name change from the Elves to Elf, at St. Alphonsus School gym in Auburn, a show which I promoted as the 18-year-old president of the church's high school youth group. I had accumulated by that point what I felt to be a whole lot of knowledge about Ronnie James Dio the musician, but that night I got to learn a lot about Ronnie the man."

"By that point, the band had grown far past being a local sensation. The first LP, *Elf* had been released, and the band was regularly playing national stages opening up for acts such as Badfinger, Edgar Winter, Cactus, Alice Cooper, Jo Jo Gunne and more. Three-hour high school dances were well in their past; they now performed the standard sets that were the norm on national stages at the time: 45 minutes for the opening act, 60 minutes for the headliner. Taking advantage of some dead time between road trips, I somehow managed to convince Valex, their Ithaca-based booking agency, to sign a contract for a full three sets/three-hour dance for less than the price they were commanding for a 45 minute show. Overjoyed at my 'coup,' I should have realized at my young age that when something sounds too good to be true, it usually is."

"The night of the big event arrived. It was a relatively small church/school gymnasium, and I had hired three extra off-duty policemen as security for the parking lot, to sweep kids either into the gym and forking over their three dollar admission, or leaving the premises and missing the show. Such was the band's popularity that the steady stream of paying customers finally abated half an hour before the end of the show."

"The road crew arrived and set up as usual, when about ten minutes before the start of the show, the head of the crew told me there was 'a problem' and I would need to meet with the group's leader: Ronnie. The band had just arrived. Somehow, it had never been communicated to them that they were expected to go back to their days of three hours of music, and the head of the crew believed the band would blow their stack when they heard. He hadn't even said a word to Ronnie, just brought me up to the side of the stage and introduced me as 'the kid in charge.' He explained to Ronnie that this was not their usual one-set show, and I nervously held the contract in my hand preparing to defend my position. I had no need. Ronnie just mildly smiled and said, 'So we'll play three hours' as nonchalantly as could be. He turned to Mickey, and said, 'Give them some piano,' and the band kicked off with 'Sit Down Honey (Everything Will Be Alright)' and never looked back."

"43 years later, people still talk about that night, and several of the photos I snapped from the side of the stage circulate around the internet."

"By this point, although all four members were of equal proficiency, something had happened that made Ronnie truly emerge as the star of the band, and the reviews were beginning to say so. At the end of the show, I was awash with joy that we had raised a lot of money for the church, and in the process had given my hometown an incredible night of music. I had a couple of shots left on my cheap, instamatic camera, and asked Ronnie if he would pose for a picture. He said, 'Sure, but let's get Mickey Lee in here too' and threw his arm around Mickey's neck and drew him in close for my photo. That's the Ronnie that I remember; gracious to an awestruck teenager, never afraid to give more than expected, and always willing to share the spotlight."

"That particular picture, unfortunately, was in poor lighting and came out unusable. Maybe what I was supposed to remember wasn't the image, but the lesson. I never saw him perform live again, but I know many people who did, and have friends who were close to Ronnie until his last days. They all describe his kindness and graciousness, and I can certainly attest to that myself. He's known for many things: the voice, the devil horns, the mystical imagery, but for me, if I had to describe Ronnie James Dio based on my brief interactions with him, I could say only one thing, 'What a gentleman!' Not a bad way to be remembered, is it?"[28]

In April of 1972, after slowly climbing up the musical ladder, Elf was given the opportunity to audition for Columbia Records. By chance, bassist Roger Glover and drummer Ian Paice of the band Deep Purple happened to be hanging at the agency office just as Ronnie and his band mate showed up. They were supposed to be on tour but as fate would have it guitarist Ritchie Blackmore had come down with hepatitis and the tour had been cancelled. Curious, Ian and Roger decided to tag along to watch Elf play. After the audition, Roger and Ian were impressed with Elf's obvious potential and Ronnie's powerful vocals.

"The dudes from Columbia (Clive Davis was one) sat in folding chairs in front of us smoking cigars," said Mickey Lee. "You could tell by looking at them that they didn't have a clue about the music. Very difficult scene for us under normal circumstances, but the Columbia boys knew who Deep Purple were. Luckily, Roger and Paice were knocked out, and I'm sure this made the decision easier for Clive and the boys. We were offered

---

[28] Article by Mike Donohue.

a deal, and with sudden time on their hands, Roger and Ian offered to produce."[29]

"I produced three albums with Elf," said Roger. "So, I knew Ronnie very well and I thought he was just a fantastic singer. He had a great voice. He was a very caring guy. He was a hard-bitten, upstate New Yorker. He could be tough and he could be cynical. He could be very funny. But his heart was pure. He loved what he did, and he always had respect for the fans. That means a lot to me."[30]

Getting an offer from Ian and Roger was a dream come true and Elf quickly accepted. Deep Purple were pioneers of heavy metal and a world-famous band that had sold millions of records. The members of Elf were all huge fans, particularly Ronnie who viewed Ritchie Blackmore as "my supreme hero."

Just a few days later, the excited band headed to Studio One in Atlanta, Georgia. Once there they began the recording process with Roger and Ian producing the record. The subsequent studio sessions which ran until July eventually yielded Elf's debut album simply titled *Elf*. The LP was released in August and featured eight original songs that had a very bluesy rock sound. The album also showcased some fantastic honky–tonk piano playing by the talented Mickey Lee Soule.

Musically, the album only hints at what Ronnie would eventually become. The song "Nevermore," perhaps more so than any of the others, gives the listener a glimpse as to the direction that Ronnie was headed, given its Dio-esque sound. For this record, Ronnie used his birth name Ronald Padavona. He did this as a way to pay tribute to his parents so that they could see their family name on at least one album. The cover featured an elf

---

[29] Padavona.com, Mickey Lee Soule interview, by Jeremy Whitted, March 2004.
[30] Interview from the official Deep Purple web site, December 13, 2013, By Something else.

with a mischievous grin which was Ronnie in costume, complete with pointy ears.

Following the release of their debut album the band was offered a spot as the support act for Deep Purple. Eagerly they accepted the gig knowing that the exposure would be great for their popularity and hopefully their record sales.

The tour lasted from August to September and then from November through December of '72. For the tour, Colin Hart was appointed as "tour manager" for Elf. Colin, who was born in South Shield, England had been in the music business for years. He had done everything from lugging equipment as a roadie to taking care of the needs of Deep Purple while they were on the road. After the tour, Colin relocated to Cortland from England at Ronnie's request so he could keep an eye on the band full time. Bruce Payne, who worked for ATI in New York, became the manager/agent for Elf during these early days.

On December 6, Elf along with Deep Purple and ZZ Top were set to play an outdoor show at Cornell University. While ZZ Top opened the show, a powerful thunderstorm rolled into the area making it too dangerous for Elf and Deep Purple to take the stage. The cancellation of the show resulted in a violent riot that left the stage and much of Deep Purple's equipment damaged.

It wasn't long after the disastrous show that Dave Feinstein dropped a bombshell and decided to quit the band. "It had nothing to with people in the band," said Dave. "We all got along really good. I decided to leave because I just needed to do some different things, you know. I went all through high school in a band and when Ronnie asked me to join his band it became my career and I hadn't really done anything in my life. I got to a point after doing that for a few years that I didn't really get a chance to experience anything that the kids in the audience were, you know, experiencing when they came to see the band. I was always the one on stage and I just wanted to do some different things, so I felt like I needed to get away from it for a while."[31]

Dave's departure was a shock to his band mates, especially Ronnie, and caused some bad feelings between the two. Despite being family, it would take several years before they would reconcile and finally speak. Dave would eventually go on to form his own band The Rods and tour with some of the biggest acts in the world, including Iron Maiden and Judas Priest. At one point a fledgling band called Metallica opened for The Rods in the early '80s.

With Dave no longer part of the lineup, Ronnie was in need of a guitar player that could match Feinstein's considerable talent. Steve Edwards, an accomplished guitarist out of Utica, New York was eventually recruited to take Dave's place. At this time, Ronnie also decided to quit playing bass so he could concentrate on his singing. Craig Gruber, a longtime friend of the band, was brought in to fill the vacated spot.

With the band repopulated, Elf continued to tour the eastern side of the United States. By the summer of '73 they had signed a new record deal with MGM Records in America and with Purple Records in the United Kingdom. Between February and March of '74, Elf was off to the UK to record their second album, at the Manor Studios. Its April UK release was under the title *Carolina Country Ball* while the American issue was *L.A./59*.

The album, like its predecessor, is heavy on the honky-tonk and boogie-rock sound. Once again, Ronnie's powerful pipes are a treat to hear and Mickey Lee's tremendous talent on the piano is outstanding throughout the LP. There is also some fine work by newcomers Steve Edwards and Craig Gruber. Steve, who had a big spot to fill when Dave left, showed that he was every bit the axeman that Dave was. His soloing is

---

[31] Dave Feinstein interview with James Curl.

top notch and his playing really stands out on "L.A.59" and "Carolina Country Ball." Gruber's bass playing helps give the album a little more of a funky element, not found on the debut, while Gary's underrated drumming is perfectly rhythmic and at times powerful.

Unlike Elf's first album, which had a more straight-ahead approach regarding its sound, *Carolina Country Ball* added a few different things like backing vocals, a string arrangement, assorted horns and a clarinet. These additions made the album's sound more complex than Elf's debut, but they worked well together and make for a fine composition.

Following the release of their new album in April of '74, Elf commenced touring with Deep Purple on a UK run that lasted until May. During this time, Ronnie and Mickey Lee collaborated on Roger Glover's solo project titled *Butterfly Ball and the Grasshopper's Feast*, a concept album based on the popular children's poem of the same name written by English poet William Roscoe. Ronnie lent his vocals to tracks 11, 19 and 20, while Mickey Lee sang on track seven.

In August of '74, Elf was back in the United States and on the tour circuit. They only played a handful of shows with Deep Purple, who then headed over to Germany for a three-month visit. Two of the concerts featured an exciting new band called Aerosmith who was attracting a lot of attention.

Continuing on without Deep Purple, Elf headlined shows in New York and Pennsylvania, sharing the stage with the J. Geils Band and Mickey Rat. Ronnie and the boys rejoined Deep Purple in November and toured throughout the United States. It was during this time that Ronnie and Ritchie Blackmore became friends. Their meshing of creative forces would lead to the formation of a band that would help define heavy metal history and create the Ronnie James Dio legend.

Chapter Four
Rainbow

Although Elf had been the warm-up act for Deep Purple for nearly three years, Ronnie and Ritchie had rarely spoken. Ronnie, knowing all about Ritchie's mercurial, and oftentimes eccentric personality, had intentionally kept his distance. The two eventually broke the ice and became fast friends over some drinks at the Rainbow club, a popular bar and grill on the Sunset Strip in Hollywood. The Rainbow was Ritchie's favorite haunt, and when in L.A. he could typically be found there carousing and drinking. "It was a place," said Ritchie "where we can have a keg of beer and a night of wickedness of the first order."[32]

As their friendship grew over the next few months, the two musicians found that they had a lot in common. Both had a love for sci-fi fantasy and medieval-based themes and lyrics. This was something that would influence Ronnie's writing style throughout his career. They also found that their sense of humor was similar, but more importantly they shared a unique musical connection. Ritchie was also a fan of Ronnie's vocals. From the first very time Blackmore had heard Ronnie sing he had been impressed with the American's distinct and powerful voice. "I felt shivers down my spine," said Ritchie speaking of the first time he had heard Ronnie.

It wasn't long after forming their friendship that Ritchie approached Ronnie about recording a single called "Black Sheep of the Family," a song originally recorded by the band Quatermass. Ritchie had proposed the song to his band mates in Deep Purple but they had rejected the idea, which upset Ritchie to no end.

Not to be thwarted, Ritchie along with Ronnie and the members of Elf went into a recording studio in Tampa

---

[32] Blackmore and Dio interview 1975 radio special, part 1.

Bay, Florida on December 12, 1974. The song turned out so well, that a few weeks later Ritchie asked Ronnie if he would be interested in recording another one. In the following days, Ronnie wrote a new song called "Sixteenth Century Greensleeves." The track was meant to be the B-side to the single, however, the single was never released. Instead, Ritchie and Ronnie decided to focus their efforts on composing an entire album and forming a new band. While drinking one night at the Rainbow club they decided to call the band Rainbow a name inspired by, and in honor of their favorite watering hole.

It was no secret in the music world that Ritchie had been unhappy playing in Deep Purple for some time. He had become disenchanted with the band's musical direction, which had started to have a "funky soul" sound, instead of the hard rock that Ritchie preferred.

By April of 1975 the guitarist's relationship with his band mates had deteriorated and his decision to quit hardly came as a surprise. His fellow members knew he was unhappy and on the verge of splitting, but they didn't know just how far he had taken his plans.

Ritchie Blackmore's Rainbow was officially announced to the music world in May of 1975. The initial lineup consisted of Ronnie on vocals, Ritchie on guitar, Mickey Lee Soule on keyboard, Craig Gruber on bass and Gary Driscoll on drums. Once the decision was final Steve Edwards' guitar services were no longer needed; his dismissal would be a precursor of things to come.

"Although I was 'fired,'" said Edwards, "I only read about my 'release' in the random notes of Rolling Stone magazine. Ronnie didn't tell me to my face or even call. I was very disappointed at the news and how it was handled."[33]

---

[33] Padavona.com

To be close to Ritchie, Ronnie and his band mates, along with Colin Hart, several crew members and Mickey Lee's wife Ramona, moved cross-country to the north end of Malibu. The band and crew shared two beachfront condos. Ritchie rented a house in Oxnard for himself and Ronnie had his own condo in the Malibu Bay Club. Once settled in, work began immediately on a new album.

When the band wasn't composing or rehearsing they would gather like a large family. Ronnie, a surprisingly good cook, would prepare authentic homemade Italian dishes.

"Ronnie's specialty," said Colin Hart, "was this fantastic Italian sauce, a giant pot of it. He got the recipe from his mom. And then Ronnie would fry up all these pork chops, sausages and fried chicken. Then he would marinade them all in the sauce; he would just toss them all in, then let them cook slowly for a few hours. It was fantastic and he was real proud of his sauce. He would cook that about once a week for the band and crew."[34]

Not long after settling in, the band decamped and headed to Europe to record their first album titled *Ritchie Blackmore's Rainbow*. Recording took place during the frigid months of February and March at the famed Musicland Studio in Munich, Germany. The album was produced by Ritchie, Ronnie and famed producer Martin Birch. Martin, who had worked with such giants as Deep Purple, Jeff Beck and Fleetwood Mac, to name a few, also mixed the album. It's interesting to note that Johann Sebastian Bach is listed among the credits.

Released on August 4, 1975 the album initially got mixed reviews. The majority of Deep Purple fans were disappointed and the Elf supporters were puzzled and caught off guard by Rainbow's unfamiliar sound. However, over time the album caught on and received great praise for its strong fantasy-themed, heroic-like

---

[34] Colin Hart interview with James Curl, December 12, 2016.

lyrical content, as well as its fresh, innovative rock 'n' roll style. In addition, the album contained a pair of gems that would help define Rainbow and become two of the band's greatest hits, "Man on the Silver Mountain," and "Catch the Rainbow." To this day, the album is acclaimed as a timeless classic, and has reached such a lofty height that it is considered one of the greatest hard rock albums of all time.

It was while the band was in the process of recording their first Rainbow album that Ronnie met Wendy Gaxiola. Wendy began working in the music industry at Decca Records while still in school in England. Essentially, she was a part-time "tea girl" but after graduating she went full time and started to learn the music business. Eventually she took a job for a different agency booking bands. Naturally intelligent, Wendy advanced quickly and began working with attorneys in the contracts department. It was some time after that she relocated to Los Angeles. Having worked in the music industry Wendy had become acquainted with a number of musicians including Blackmore and the members of Deep Purple.

While in L.A. she ran into Ritchie and his wife Babs at the Rainbow club. Happy to see her, Ritchie invited her to a party at his house in the Hollywood Hills. While attending the party Wendy was introduced to the singer for Rainbow, Ronnie James Dio. With long blond hair, vivid hazel eyes and strikingly beautiful features, Ronnie was smitten; pursuit began shortly thereafter.

Initially, Wendy thought that Ronnie was a bit short for her, but the singer's persistence paid off. The two began dating and eventually fell in love. "I fell in love with his brain and his humor and everything about him. He had a very good sense of humor,"[35] said Wendy.

---

[35] *The Other Side of Rainbow*, by Greg Prato, CreateSpace Independent Publishing Platform (November 4, 2016).

With Rainbow's debut album completed, Ronnie and the boys returned to Malibu to begin rehearsals for an upcoming tour. Unfortunately, things didn't turn out as expected.

"Even at rehearsals," said Colin Hart, "I knew the signs of discontent in Ritchie were surfacing. He has this thing he does which, although he says nothing, his actions shout, reverberating around the room. He simply stops playing, slowly turns round, slips his guitar over his head and lays it on top of the stack, switches off and walks slowly and silently away."[36]

It was then that Ritchie began his methodical termination of the Elf members. The first casualty was bassist Craig Gruber. Ritchie and Craig had been at odds since the inception of Rainbow. Craig felt that Ritchie had broken up Elf for his own gains, and his aversion toward Blackmore showed.

As Mickey Lee Soule remembers, this is how the events unfolded. "Basically the way that it happened, was that when the bass player left he hadn't really been a member of Elf as long as the rest of us, and Ronnie who was the leader of the band, so to speak, got myself and the drummer aside and said, 'Look, Ritchie wants to get rid of the bass player; he wants to replace him and there is not much that we can do about it but we will make a pact between the three of us that we will all stick together.' And so, I said, 'Yeah, okay, sure.' But then a couple of weeks later Ronnie approached me and said, 'Well, now Ritchie wants to replace the drummer and there is not much that we can do about it but let's make a pact between you and me that we are going to stick together.' And then right there I knew that the old days were over."

"I had an opportunity at that time to do something different and I went to Europe and played on one of

---

[36] *A Hart Life*, by Colin Hart and Dick Allix, Wymer Publishing (October 3, 2011).

Roger Glover's albums and I did a tour with the Ian Gillan Band and a couple of other things, so I basically left Rainbow on my own, but I was probably going to be the next one on the list to get the axe anyway. I wasn't getting the creative input that I wanted from it and there were a lot of things going on at that time, personally, in my life. I had just had a son and I was pretty fed up with the business side of things and the way that all of us had been treated by various record companies and things and there was a lot of drugs going on at the time so I basically just got fed up with the whole thing after a while and just got out of the music business completely for almost ten years."

"I ended up doing some other things, got involved in the theater and whatever but that is basically what happened to the first Rainbow. We never did get out on the road. The drummer was replaced by Cozy and I am not even sure who replaced me; it might have been Don Airey, I can't remember exactly who was next in line but that is why you are not going to hear anything live by that band."[37]

Throughout the process of sacking the members of Elf, Ronnie was very upset with Ritchie. These were guys that he had grown up with and had played with for years—Elf was a family. But what could he do? It was Ritchie's band and Ronnie had very little say. When Ronnie confronted Ritchie, the guitarist cited that his decision was due to Driscoll's style of drumming and the funk-style bass playing of Gruber. Whatever Ritchie's reasons, Ronnie learned quickly that being in Rainbow was a business, and that business could be cutthroat.

To replace the Elf members, Ritchie recruited the great English drummer Cozy Powell, who had made his name playing with the likes of Sorcerer and Jeff Beck. The hard-living Scottish born Jimmy Bain from the band Harlot was recruited to take over bass duties. And to fill

---

[37] Padavona.com

in on the keyboard spot, Ritchie hired Julliard School of Music graduate Tony Carey, a talented yet virtual unknown.

"Ritchie heard my band [Blessings] playing at a rehearsal studio in Hollywood," recalled Tony. "And at the time he was auditioning people for the Rainbow road crew. I was 20, I guess. So the timing was perfect for me to leave this band, because I couldn't see our record getting finished." So when Ritchie approached Tony and asked him if he would like to join Rainbow, Tony said, "Sure. I'd love to." It gave Tony a way to get out of the situation he was in.

On November 10, 1975 the new lineup of Rainbow embarked on a world tour starting in Montreal, Canada. The centerpiece of the band's live performance was a computer-controlled rainbow with 4,000 multicolored lightbulbs that stretched 40 feet across the stage. The idea was dreamt up by Ronnie and Ritchie. Visually speaking, the rainbow was a great idea, but at times the electrical interference played havoc with Ritchie's amps and several shows had to be canceled after only a few songs. Having such a visually stunning stage set, when it worked correctly, Rainbow quickly became known for their spectacular and powerful live performances.

Following a successful first tour, the members of Rainbow began composing their second album, *Rainbow Rising*. Alternately referred to as *Rising*, the album would quickly become known as a masterpiece that captured the band at the peak of their creative and physical powers.

Recording once again took place at Musicland studios in Germany. The album was released to eager fans on May 17, 1976 and was an instant hit. Although only clocking in at a relatively short 33 minutes, the album more than makes up for its lack of time with a collection of terrific songs. Standing out above the rest is "Stargazer," an epic eight-minute composition. The song opens with Cozy's short, yet powerful drum solo that gives the listener a small taste of the drummer's immense, unerring talent that has been called "a great drumming moment."[38]

From there, Ronnie's evocative vocals tell the story of a wizard whose attempt to fly, by constructing a tower to the stars, leads to the enslavement of vast numbers of people. The song features the Munich Philharmonic Orchestra, a Vako Orchestron, and what Blackmore called, "a string thing all playing this half-Turkish scale."[39] Blackmore's solo, after the second verse, is in *B Phrygian dominant scale*, and is cited as "one of his best."[40]

"The song has been called a 'morality tale' and its lyrics are written from the standpoint of 'a slave in Egyptian times,' according to lyricist Ronnie James Dio. They relate the story of the wizard, an astronomer who becomes 'obsessed with the idea of flying' and enslaves a vast army of people to build him a tower from which he can take off and fly.[41] The people hope for the day when their misery comes to an end, building the tower in harsh conditions ("In the heat and rain, with whips and chains; just to see him fly, too many died").

"In the end, the wizard climbs to the top of the tower but instead of flying, falls down and dies: 'No sound as he falls instead of rising. Time standing still, then there's blood on the sand.'"[42]

The next song, "A Light in the Black," continues the story of the people who have lost all purpose after the

---

[38] Litten, Robert, *Famous DRUM FILLS, Licks & Solos!*, www.DrumsTheWord.com. p. 372.

[39] *Perkins, Jeff. Rainbow - Uncensored on the Record. Coda Books. p. 70. ISBN 9781908538574.*

[40] *Maloof, Rich; Prown, Pete (2006). Shred! The Ultimate Guide to Warp-speed Guitar. Backbeat Books. pp. 32–33. ISBN 9780879308773.*

[41] *Perkins, Jeff. Rainbow - Uncensored on the Record. Coda Books. p. 70. ISBN 9781908538574.*

[42] Wikipedia, *Stargazer* (Rainbow song).

wizard's death "until they see the light in the dark," according to Dio."[43]

Rising received great critical acclaim upon its release, and to this day stands out as a truly iconic album. The UK-based magazine, *Kerrang!* ranked *Rising* as, "the greatest heavy metal album of all time." Rob Halford of Judas Priest called it, "a significant record" and a "thrilling album." Halford also claimed that, "It plays as well and sounds as well and feels as good now as when it first came out. That shows you how important and how valuable that music still is."[44]

With the popularity of *Rainbow Rising*, the band embarked on a world tour that began in Europe near the end of August 1976. It was quickly evident that Rainbow's fan base and popularity had grown exponentially since their last outing; almost every show was sold out. From Europe the band headed to Australia and finally finished up in Japan near the end of the year.

In early 1977 there was trouble in the Rainbow camp that led to Jimmy Bain being fired. The command came down from Ritchie and was executed by Ritchie's tour manager Bruce Payne. Reasons coming out of the Rainbow camp were varied. Some said it was because of Jimmy's excessive partying and alcohol consumption. Others because he was playing out of tune. And yet another was that Jimmy did not complement the style and direction of the founding members.

"There was never really a specific reason given," said Colin Hart. "Even Jimmy couldn't get a reason out of Ritchie when he asked him directly. He sure did like to party a lot and perhaps that did play some part in it but, in the end, I think it was just Ritchie's pursuit of the perfect lineup."[45]

---

[43] Perkins, Jeff. *Rainbow - Uncensored on the Record.* Coda Books. p. 70. ISBN 9781908538574.
[44] Booth, Alison. "RAINBOW "Rising" At 40: Interview with Rob Halford." Metal Shock Finland. Retrieved 22 June 2016.
[45] Colin Hart interview with James Curl, December 12, 2016.

Whatever the reason, the Rainbow revolving door had been opened, and it would continue to swing both ways for years to come.

To replace Jimmy, Ritchie called his friend Mark Clarke and offered him the job as bass player. Clarke, who at the time had just left his band Natural Gas, accepted the position eagerly.

From May to July of 1977 the band was in France working on their third LP, *Long Live Rock 'n' Roll*. The album was recorded at Château d'Hérouville, an 18th century castle-like manor house-built in 1740. The place got its affectionate nickname "Honky Château," from the title of one of the three records Elton John recorded at the facility. Other artists who recorded at the place include David Bowie, Pink Floyd, Fleetwood Mac, the Bee Gees and Cat Stevens. The Chateau was also famous for having served as a summer home for Polish-born composer Fredrick Chopin.

The band playfully called it "Horrorsville" because it was allegedly haunted. While recording the album, there were a lot of strange occult things that went on. Some of these "strange occurrences" may have been perpetuated by the band, who at the time, was dabbling in black magic and holding nightly séances. Ritchie, who was convinced that the place was haunted by a demon named Baal, was the ring-leader. He and Ronnie along with Ritchie's girlfriend and Wendy would set up a table with a Ouija board in the center and conduct séances. Colin Hart, Martin Birch and Tony Carey refused to get involved.

"The most memorable thing about recording the album," said Ronnie, "was the occult things we went through. We went through a severe phase of contacting a spirit that was the most scary thing I think any of us ever been through. We rose the spirit named Baal." According to Ronnie, Baal was really chaotic in trying to stop the recording of the album. While recording, said Ronnie, "Tape machines would suddenly stop. Doors that were locked that had only had one key to one person we trusted, we'd go up there and things would be playing."[46]

Toward the end of recording the album said Ronnie, "My wife Wendy got pushed down the stairs and accused me of it. I was walking down the stairs, Cozy was behind me, Wendy was probably five or six stairs ahead of me, luckily she had a box of China, antique China we had bought, and suddenly she tumbled down the stairs and landed on the box of China, thank God because it broke her fall, only broke a couple plates."[47]

Wendy then turned around and yelled at Ronnie saying, "You bastard, you pushed me!"[48] Ronnie of course denied it, and looked to Cozy who confirmed that Ronnie had not touched Wendy. "That was Baal," said Ronnie.

Besides séances there were lots of pranks being played by the band and crew members alike. Although Ronnie got great joy out of the shenanigans he was seldom involved. The majority were played out by Ritchie and Cozy, and the more sadistic the more Ritchie and his drummer liked it.

Many of the pranks were directed towards Tony. Pretentious at times, Tony apparently rubbed Ritchie the wrong way. It also didn't help that Tony liked to experiment with drugs; something Ritchie was against. As a result he elicited Ritchie's ire.

Because of the consistent pranks, Tony became increasingly isolated, preferring to stay in his room when not recording. One particularly revolting prank was to sneak into Tony's room and leave a human turd on the keyboard player's nightstand.

"Ritchie was a bit relentless with his practical jokes on poor old Tony," said Colin. "Woe betide him, if he left his window open during the night as he would be

---

[46] YouTube interview Eric Blair, part 4.
[15] Ibid.
[48] Ibid.

visited by the nerveless drummer who was completely unfazed by heights and would think nothing of going over the roof into Tony's room and leaving something unmentionable or removing certain items."[49]

One night, finally having had enough of jokes and séances, Tony packed his belongings and quit the band.

"I left," said Tony. "I left actually in the middle of the night in a taxi. 'Get me out of here,' kind of thing. I fled the Chateau."[50] The incident inspired Ronnie and Ritchie to write the song "L.A. Connection," which came out on the album.

Following Tony's departure Mark Clarke gave notice that he would be cutting out as well. From the start he and Ritchie had been at odds with the way Mark played his bass. Most of the time Mark played with his fingers and Ritchie preferred a bass player that used a pick. Mark also had a habit of bending the neck of his bass while playing that would indeed throw the instrument out of tune. Ritchie, who could not tolerate bad musicianship, would get infuriated and the confrontations between the two escalated, going from bad to worse. At one point Ritchie took Mark's bass and recorded the bass parts for several of the tracks himself. The conflict eventually ended with an unhappy Clarke leaving.

Suddenly short a bass player and keyboardist, the band decided to suspend recording and fly to L.A. to hold auditions. Despite Ritchie's fearsome reputation as a hard guy to work for, there was no shortage of musicians willing to share the stage with him. Unsatisfied with the crop of keyboardists that showed up, Ritchie eventually flew in David Stone who had played in Symphonic Slam.

After looking at approximately 40 different bass players, Ritchie decided on Australian-born Bob Daisley. Bob was an exceptional and well-known bass player, having spent time in Chicken Shack, Mungo

---

[49] Ibid.
[50] *The Other Side of Rainbow*, by Greg Prato, CreateSpace Independent Publishing Platform (November 4, 2016).

Jerry and Widowmaker. At his audition Bob hit it off with the band. More importantly he was just what Ritchie wanted—a bass player that played with a pick.

With the band repopulated, rehearsals commenced at Pirate Sound studio in L.A., but ended quickly. Ritchie, holding to his unpredictable nature, suddenly announced that he wanted to move to the East Coast. Ever at the ready, Colin Hart was dispatched with instructions to find suitable places to rent for Ritchie and Cozy. Ronnie and Wendy rented a place in New Canaan, Connecticut.

No sooner did everyone get settled into their new surrounding when they had to repack and head out for the *On Stage* world tour. The tour was named after their double live album that was issued in July of '77. The album was released after only two studio albums; an audacious move that raised some eyebrows in the industry.

The tour began on September 23, 1977 traveling across Sweden, Norway, Denmark and Holland. By now Rainbow was huge and bringing in massive crowds. In some parts of the world they were as big as, if not bigger than, Deep Purple, especially in Europe where Ritchie was loved by his adoring fans. Near the end of November, the band halted their tour in Wales and returned to the Chateau to finish recording *Long Live Rock 'n' Roll*.

Having finally completed the album, Rainbow took off on a 17-date tour that began in Nagoya, Japan on January 11, 1978. In Japan, Rainbow was extremely popular and each venue was filled to overflowing with excited fans.

Following the Japanese tour Rainbow returned to America for a three-month hiatus. During the time off Ronnie and Wendy were married in New Canaan, Connecticut on April 7, 1978. In attendance were Ronnie and Wendy's families, road crew and friends.

The wedding party consisted of Bruce Payne as best man, Ritchie, Raymond D'Addario, Bob Daisley,

Ronnie's son Danny and Colin Hart. Happily wedded, the couple left for their honeymoon shortly thereafter.

Two days later on April 9, *Long Live Rock 'n' Roll* was released. The album featured a collection of outstanding tunes like "Long Live Rock 'n' Roll," "Kill the King," "Gates of Babylon" and "Rainbow Eyes," a song Ronnie wrote about Wendy's eyes, because at times they seemed to change colors.

Sadly, the album would be the last to feature Ronnie on vocals. In many fans' opinions, it is the last great album that Rainbow ever did, despite going on to have impressive chart-topping success in the post-Dio era.

For some time the storm clouds of discontent had been gathering in the Rainbow camp. By December of 1978 Ronnie's unhappiness with Ritchie had reached a breaking point. It was no secret that Blackmore wanted to change the sound and musical direction of Rainbow. He made it clear that he wanted the next album to be more "mainstream." Ritchie wanted to get away from the sword and sorcery-themed music and heavy metal sound. His new idea was to take the band into a more commercialized direction; Ritchie desired the FM radio market and was hell-bent on getting it.

The new direction was something to which Ronnie was vehemently opposed. As a result of their conflicting musical visions, Ronnie decided it was time to leave the band. But, before he could make it official Bruce Payne phoned Ronnie in December to tell him that Ritchie was breaking up Rainbow and would only be keeping Cozy. The news didn't surprise Ronnie; however he was none too happy with the way the split went down. The singer felt that he was "pushed before he had time to jump."[51]

Following Ronnie's exit, Bob Daisley was the next to be let go a few months later. Dave Stone hung in for a while longer, but without Ronnie in the band his

---

[51] *A Hart Life*, by Colin Hart and Dick Allix, Wymer Publishing (October 3, 2011).

enthusiasm quickly dried up, so he ended up walking away.

Ensuing rumors followed as to why Ronnie had left Rainbow. Ritchie claimed (in *The Ritchie Blackmore Story* DVD) that Ronnie left because he was upset about a Circus magazine cover photo that only showed Ritchie and not the other members of Rainbow. According to Wendy Dio, "Ronnie was fired by Blackmore because he refused to write commercial songs."[52]

It wasn't just the musical direction that caused Ronnie to leave Rainbow. The singer's discontent and resentment had been building for quite some time. Ronnie, who was always gracious and giving with his fans, would normally stay after each show to sign autographs, sometimes for hours. Ritchie on the other hand was smug. He would typically leave right after each show and rarely signed autographs. Ronnie found his band mate's treatment of his fans insufferable.

When news of Ronnie's split became public it was a shock to fans, but their disappointment was short-lived. Rainbow, as Ritchie desired, would rebuild and indeed conquer the FM market. As for Ronnie, some of his greatest work was about to be created.

---

[52] UltimateGuitar.com, interview with Wendy Dio, June 23, 2011.

Chapter Five
Black Sabbath

No longer a member of Rainbow, Ronnie returned to L.A. where he briefly focused his attention on a solo career. For a time, he and David Stone worked together on material that would eventually become solo Dio songs. But for now fate had other plans for the singer.

About the time Ronnie was contemplating a solo career, Black Sabbath was having trouble of its own. By early 1979 the band was beginning to fall apart and was in a state of chaos. Their charismatic front-man, Ozzy Osbourne, had quit, leaving his band mates, Tony Iommi, Geezer Butler and Bill Ward to wonder what they were going to do. They were, however, not without a singer for long.

Black Sabbath was formed in 1968 in Birmingham, England. Not wanting to be stuck in dreary factory jobs for the next 40 years Ozzy, Tony, Bill and Geezer got into playing music as a "way out" and dreamed of making it big and becoming famous rock stars. Initially, after playing in other bands, the boys came together and formed a group called Earth Blues Company, which was later shortened to Earth.

As they played gigs and wrote songs the band developed a unique sound in large part brought on by Tony's guitar playing. While working in a factory at the age of 17, Tony had the tips of his middle fingers on his fretting hand severed. To compensate for his missing digits, the resourceful guitarist fabricated a pair of plastic fingertips from dish detergent bottles that he melted down, shaped and wrapped in leather. He then retuned his guitar by using lighter gauge strings to make bending the strings easier. The resulting sound was extremely heavy. Coupled with Ozzy's vocals, Geezer's bass and Bill's thunderous drums, the band created a truly distinctive sound.

Things really started to happen for the band when Geezer came up with an idea for a song that was inspired by a strange incident. Having an interest in horror movies and the occult, Geezer had been reading black magic-themed books and the weekly magazine, Man, Myth and Magic. One night he saw what he believed to be the apparition of a black shadow figure standing at the foot of his bed. After telling his band mates about the frightening experience they worked on composing a song about the dark visitor, entitling it "Black Sabbath," after the 1963 Boris Karloff film.

Audience reaction to the song was immediate and the boys knew they were onto something special. This also led to the band changing its name to Black Sabbath. It was a name that fit perfectly. With their heavy riff-laden songs, mythological-themed and satanic-inspired lyrics, the name embodied the dark mystique of the band and what they were about musically.

Over time Sabbath, along with Deep Purple and Led Zeppelin, have become widely regarded as the progenitors of heavy metal; in short, one of the bands that invented heavy metal. Their importance and impact to the history of heavy metal and hard rock cannot be overstated. Sabbath were pioneers of their time, and originators of what many people term "doom metal." With such iconic albums as, *Black Sabbath*, *Paranoid* and *Master of Reality*, they helped create and define an entire genre of music.

It was while attending a party at Don Arden's house that Ronnie first met Tony Iommi. The two were introduced by Sharon Arden, the daughter of Don Arden, who was managing Sabbath at the time. Although not involved with Ozzy yet, Sharon would eventually go on to marry Ozzy and become the well-known television personality Sharon Osbourne.

"It was at this point that Sharon introduced me to Ronnie," said Tony. "I approached him and said, 'I'm in a terrible situation. I don't think it's going to work anymore with what we got. Would you be interested in doing something else?"[53]

Ronnie was definitely interested, but it would take several months before he and Tony would actually get together. Tony, Geezer and Bill were still in a state of confusion as to what was going to happen with Ozzy and didn't know if he was going to return or not. Finally, after Ozzy made his departure official, Tony said to Bill and Geezer. "Why don't we try Ronnie?"

A few days later Ronnie got a call from Tony who invited the singer over to his house for a jam session. Pulling up in his big Cadillac, Tony got a laugh when he realized that Ronnie had to have the seat moved all the way forward.

At Tony's house Ronnie became acquainted with Bill and Geezer. While getting to know the Sabbath members Tony played Ronnie a song he had been working on called "Children of the Sea." In no time, Ronnie came up with a vocal melody for it. "Tony had this great riff he played me," said Ronnie, "but nothing to go with it. I said, 'Gimme a minute' and went into the corner and started writing down the words. Then we recorded it. When we played it back it was obvious to both of us, we really had something here."[54]

Tony, Bill and Geezer were pleased to say the least. "We were really impressed," said Tony, "because within a day we'd gone from nothing happening for ages to being able to come up with a song immediately. We played a bit of 'Lady Evil', and Ronnie immediately sang to that as well. We thought bloody hell, we're onto a winner here."[55]

Despite the great progress that Ronnie and his new band mates were making, Geezer decided that he would have to leave the band. For some time now he had been

---

[53] Ironman, *My Journey Through Heaven and Hell with Black Sabbath*, by Tony Iommi with T.J. Lammers, Da Capo Press, 2011.
[54] YouTube interview.
[55] Ibid.

having marital problems and he could no longer avoid dealing with them. So, he headed home.

Until a replacement could be found Ronnie picked up the bass and work on the album continued. A short time later Tony brought in his friend Geoff Nicholls from the band Quartz as a temporary replacement.

The first song that the four worked on together was "Heaven and Hell," a song that Tony had been working on previously. Tony played Ronnie the riff and, "Ronnie just sang away to it," said Tony. "It was that instantaneous. And we said to each other, oh man, do we like this."[56]

With Ronnie in the band there was a new dynamic and new sense of purpose that reinvigorated his band mates. And it was easy to see that together Ronnie and Tony created a genuinely great writing partnership. Ronnie's ideas were refreshing and vibrant and helped lift Sabbath out of the rut it had been in for some time. In fact, Tony felt that Sabbath had gotten a little lazy over the past few years and he liked what he was seeing and hearing. Ronnie challenged them and as a result Tony felt that the band was getting progressively tighter and more professional.

Everyone was pleased with the progress on the *Heaven and Hell* album except Don Arden. Don had made it clear that the band needed to get Ozzy back and that he didn't like the idea of having Ronnie as the singer. "You can't have a midget singing for Black Sabbath," said Don. Ronnie and Tony knew, however, that they were onto something good and had no intention of stopping. So, out of spite, Don had the rented furniture removed from the house that Tony and Bill were staying in.

Realizing that the situation was only going to get worse, Tony decided to cut his relationship with Don and move on. After some talks with Ronnie and Bill it was

---

[56] Ibid.

agreed that it was time for a change. A few weeks later Sabbath left Los Angeles and relocated to Miami, Florida, where they rented a house owned by Bee Gees front-man Barry Gibb. In no time, they had a rehearsal studio set up and work continued. To help out, Ronnie had his old band mate from Rainbow and Elf, Craig Gruber come down and play bass while Geoff became the official keyboard player. But this lineup didn't last long. Geezer, having sorted out his marital problems, was back in the band a few weeks later to resume his rightful spot as bass player. A few weeks after his return, writing for the album was completed and it was ready to be recorded.

Heaven and Hell was recorded at Criteria Studios in Miami, and was produced by Martin Birch. Martin was a familiar face to Ronnie. Not only had he produced several albums from some big bands, he had also produced *Ritchie Blackmore's Rainbow* and *Rising*, as well as subsequent Rainbow albums.

With the release of *Heaven and Hell* in April of 1980, Black Sabbath showed that they were still a force to be reckoned with. Despite having a different sound than classic Sabbath, overall the album received a positive reception from fans and became their highest charting release since 1975's *Sabotage*, as well as their third bestselling album behind *Paranoid* and *Master of Reality*, respectively.

With new album and a positive outlook, Sabbath embarked on a tour of the UK and Europe. They hit the stage in Aurich, Germany for their first show with Ronnie on April 17, 1980. Understandably they were a little apprehensive. Black Sabbath without Ozzy Osbourne was considered by many to be heavy metal sacrilege. Ozzy had been such an integral and compelling part of Sabbath that everyone wondered, would the fans accept Ronnie?

Confident as usual, Ronnie took to the stage. At the helm, he belted out the lyrics of a varied set consisting of classics like "War Pigs" and "Paranoid" as well as material from the new album. Although the initial show went over well, there were some fans who found it hard to accept Ronnie.

Tony spoke of the tour saying, "We were doing big shows, and it was difficult for Ronnie to go out and stand in front of people who had seen Ozzy in that spot for ten years. Some of the kids hated it and they shouted, 'Ozzy, Ozzy!'"[57]

"But eventually, Ronnie won them over."[58]

Part of the stage show's production featured a cross that flashed multi-colored lights in different sequences. When the band played "Heaven and Hell" the cross was supposed to burst into flames, but at times it wouldn't work as designed. During a show at Madison Square Garden the band experienced what can only be described as a Spinal Tap moment. Ronnie did his big build-up, saying to the audience, "I want you all to concentrate on the cross." Over and over he told the crowd, "Keep concentrating." When he got to the crescendo the cross was supposed to burst into spectacular flames, but instead it just fizzled out like a "little sparkler," which prompted Ronnie to say, "Well, I guess you're not concentrating enough."[59]

It was during his time in Sabbath that Ronnie popularized his now legendary hand gesture known as "the devil horns." The beloved fan salute however had a very different meaning to Ronnie.

"My grandmother, who came from Italy, didn't speak a lot of English, so she was quite imbued with the superstitions that people had in that area for a long time. We'd walk down the street when I was a little kid and she would raise those two fingers if someone was walking on the other side of the street. I asked her one day, 'What

---

[57] Ironman, My Journey Through Heaven and Hell with Black Sabbath, by Tony Iommi with T.J. Lammers, Da Capo Press, 2011.
[58] Ibid.
[59] Ibid.

are you doing?' She said, 'I'm protecting you from the evil eye.' And I thought, '*That's cool.*' Okay, the horns. 'What's it called?' The malocchio. We used to say, 'Give them the malocchio' and we'd raise the fingers up. I did it so much onstage that I've become synonymous with it, as if I invented it. I keep saying that some guy named Ogg about 100,000 years ago raised those two fingers up, and it probably meant something to him as well, so we'll have to give Ogg the credit for the creation."

During one interview Ronnie said of his famous rock 'n' roll symbol, "I doubt very much if I would be the first one who ever did that. That's like saying I invented the wheel; I'm sure someone did that at some other point. I think you'd have to say that I made it fashionable. I used it so much and all the time and it had become my trademark until the Britney Spears audience decided to do it as well. So, it kind of lost its meaning with that. But it was... I was in Sabbath at the time. It was a symbol that I thought was reflective of what that band was supposed to be all about. It's *not* the devil's sign like we're here with the devil. It's to ward off the 'evil eye' or to give the 'evil eye,' depending on which way you do it. It's just a symbol, but it had magical incantations and attitudes to it and I felt it worked very well with Sabbath. So I became very noted for it and then everybody else started to pick up on it and away it went. But I would never say I take credit for being the first to do it. I say because I did it so much that it became the symbol of rock 'n' roll of some kind."[60]

Ronnie's first cousin Bill Padavona remembers the first time he and Ronnie witnessed their grandmother use the malocchio.

"There was an old woman that lived just a few houses from Ronnie's house," said Bill. "She was an old Sicilian lady, always wore black—black socks, black bun in her hair. I remember her first name was Concetta, and my

---

[60] *"Dio - Interviewed by EvilG" Metal-Rules.com. March 9, 2001.*

grandmother always said Concetta was like the local 'witch doctor.' And Ronnie and I were sitting on the front porch of our grandmother's house and she went by and she was barking off something in Italian and I guess our grandmother didn't like what she said, so she gave her the 'evil eye,' the finger thing to ward her off. So then Ronnie and I picked up on it and we would do it to people we didn't like; we were just kids. So that's how that whole thing really got going."[61]

Sabbath returned to America in July to begin their run of the States. They toured up until August and were scheduled to play a show in Denver when Bill unexpectedly up and quit. For some time, he had been drinking excessively, even while playing gigs, which was something he never used to do. His drinking was also breaking him down physically, causing him to have panic attacks and become angry and aggressive.

"It was August 21, 1980. We were due to do a gig in Denver," said Tony, "but he got absolutely legless, got in his bus with his brother Jim driving, and just cleared off. We didn't even know he was gone until someone told us, 'Bill has left.'"[62] The Denver gig had to be cancelled.

When Bill was finally contacted, he said that he didn't want to do it anymore. This concerned Ronnie greatly because he and Bill were friends. "We've got to get him back," said a worried Ronnie.

Bill's unexpected exit was a shock and sent the band into a panic, particularly Tony. Sabbath was scheduled to headline a huge open-air festival in Hawaii in just about a week; if they didn't find a suitable replacement quickly, the show would have to be cancelled.

With no time to waste, Ronnie and Tony started the hunt. They had gotten a number of demo tapes from various drummers one of them being Vinny Appice.

---

[61] Bill Padavona interview with James Curl.
[62] Ironman, My Journey Through Heaven and Hell with Black Sabbath, by Tony Iommi with T.J. Lammers, Da Capo Press, 2011.

Tony had also acquired the album *It's a Circus World* by Vinny's band Axis and liked what he heard. Moreover, Ronnie was familiar with Vinny, who had recorded albums with Rick Derringer. Vinny's older brother Carmine was also known to Ronnie and was a well-established drummer having played with Vanilla Fudge, Jeff Beck and Rod Stewart.

After some discussion, Ronnie said, "Let's get in touch with him."[63] Tony agreed. It would be Vinny or no one else. If they liked him he was in. If they didn't, there would be no time to get another drummer.

Over at the Appice home, Vinny got a call from Tony's tour manager telling him that Black Sabbath was looking for a drummer. He was then asked if he would like to come down to the hotel and meet Tony. Excited by the prospect of playing with Black Sabbath, Vinny readily agreed. The next day he met up with Tony and the preliminary meeting went well. The two agreed to meet up the following day at SIR Studio on the Sunset Strip so Vinny could audition.

It was at SIR that Vinny first met Ronnie and Geezer. Right from the start Ronnie and Vinny hit it off and became fast friends. "When I first met him we started talking," said Vinny. "We're both Italian, we're both from New York, he's from upstate, I'm from Brooklyn. And we just bonded, we liked the same foods, he's a finicky eater and so am I and we just got all these things in common, so we really hit it off well."[64]

Setting up his drums Tony was worried because Vinny's set was considerably smaller than Bill's huge kit. In fact, the whole idea of working with another drummer had Tony absolutely flustered; he and Bill had been together for years, even before they played in Black Sabbath.

---

[63] Ironman, My Journey Through Heaven and Hell with Black Sabbath, by Tony Iommi with T.J. Lammers, Da Capo Press, 2011.
[64] Vinny Appice on Black Sabbath pranks, YouTube interview, April 25, 2012.

The first song the group played together was "Neon Nights," and it was quickly apparent that Vinny was a great drummer and gelled well with the rest of the band. After playing a few more songs the decision was easy—Vinny was in.

For the next two days Vinny did his best to learn the set list, but with the rushed schedule he really didn't have enough time to become 100% familiar with each song. To help, he made what was essentially a "cheat sheet" containing notes for each song, and then headed to Hawaii.

At the show, Vinny showed up with his "tiny little kit" packed in the back seat and trunk of a car. This troubled Tony greatly. He had assumed that Vinny would show up with a bigger kit for the gig and now he was worried that with his small kit no one would be able to hear him. "I really went to bits back stage," said Tony, "pacing up and down and Ronnie said, 'It'll be all right.'"

As it turned out Vinny's drums sounded great, but unfortunately it rained during the show and his notes got smudged, so he was unable to read them. As a result, he was forced to "wing it" for most of the set.

"He didn't know where we were," said Tony, "but he did really good."[65] After the show Vinny took his soggy notes, autographed them and threw them out into the audience.

Having made it through the Hawaii show, Sabbath toured the States for three more months, then played five shows in Japan during November. Their next stop was Australia for four shows, before heading to the UK in December where they took a well-deserved break from their demanding schedule. It was during this time that Warner Brothers approached Sabbath about doing a song for the upcoming animated movie, *Heavy Metal*. So, during a break the guys stayed with Ringo Starr who was

---

[65] Ibid.

now the owner of the late John Lennon's mansion, John having been murdered only a few weeks before. While staying at the house Vinny was offered Lennon's personal bedroom, but he refused. Having worked with the famous Beatle a few years before, Vinny was the only member of Sabbath that had a connection to John and the idea of staying in his room spooked him.

It was at the house that Sabbath wrote and recorded the song "The Mob Rules" as well as the track "E5150" which is in the movie but was not included on the soundtrack album. For recording they set Vinny's drums up in the hallway and used John's recording studio called "The White Room." They would eventually re-record "The Mob Rules" when they returned to L.A. Ronnie said about the *Heaven and Hell* tour, "It was an excellent tour. I think we were probably riding quite high on the *Heaven and Hell* success, and so we ended up playing really, really well. Even towards the end of the shows, we were still great."

Yet even with their success there was tension building between Ronnie and his band mates. They were slowly slipping into a state of turmoil and beginning to break apart.

Once back in L.A. the band rented a house in Toluca Lake where they finished writing and recording *Mob Rules* at the Record Plant Studios. Recording sessions went smoothly and the record was released on November 4, 1981. From the album sprang two outstanding songs, "Turn up the Night" and "The Sign of the Southern Cross." A subsequent tour ensued that took the band from North America to Europe, lasting from November of '81 until August of '82.

During the tour there was at least one Spinal Tap story worthy of mentioning. Speaking of the incident Vinny said, "One time with Black Sabbath, we were playing the song 'Black Sabbath.' Whenever something weird happens, it's during that song. It's weird. The weather would start... So we're playing in England... Stafford...

10,000 people, sold out, in an arena. Back then we used smoke during the show, and they put dry ice in a big oil drum barrel full of water. That's how you created smoke back then. Now it's like a little box. Back then, you had to have these barrels and they'd throw the ice in and hoses."

"So we were playing the song, and we were in the low part, and they put the ice in and the freaking thing explodes behind me. So the water goes up 25 feet in the air, and everybody's, like, 'Yeah!' thinking that's part of the show. But it exploded, and all the water and the ice comes down on the drums and me. And they go, 'Holy shit!' And the drums are like, [*makes thumping sound*]. And the band's laughing; Tony loved it, Ronnie was laughing, Geezer… It was hilarious. And I'm sitting there, and then all of a sudden, my ass is burning. I was, like, 'What the fuck?' Dry ice went down the crack of my pants and it's burning, 'cause it sticks to your skin. And I'm like, 'Oh, shit!' 10,000 people, and I said, 'I'll be right back.' I went off the stage to the medics, and the stuff was stuck to my ass."

"The medics were two women. 'Okay, pull your pants down. We're gonna take that off.' So we all came off stage. They had to wipe up the stage and all that. And they put cream on me, they put bandages. They're asking me, 'Do you wanna go? Can you play the rest of the set? If you can't, cancel it.' The place is sold out. I said, 'Of course.' So I went up with a pillow. And we continued and played the whole set."[66]

Following the *Mob Rules* tour Sabbath returned to Los Angles and began working on *Live Evil*, a live album with recordings taken from shows in Dallas, San Antonio and Seattle during the *Mob Rules* world tour. However, there were problems that had been festering for months in the band. There were rumors of Ronnie and Vinny

---

[66] Blabber Mouth, Vinny Appice recalls getting his ass burned on stage with Black Sabbath, June 9, 2016.

doing a solo album behind the backs of Tony and Geezer. In fact, because of the success of the *Heaven and Hell* album, Ronnie had been offered a solo deal from Warner Brothers. The news didn't go over too well with Tony or Geezer. As a result of the gossip and unspoken accusations, tension in the band was high and on the verge of erupting.

Vinny, who could see the signs of trouble while the band was on tour said, "I knew things were coming to a close from some of the things that were happening on the road. Ronnie and I would ride in one car, Geezer and Tony in another car, and everybody was breaking away from each other a little bit."

It was during the mixing of *Live Evil* that the cracks finally gave way. Lee De Carlo, who was the brother of Yvonne De Carlo, the actress who played Lily Munster on the TV show The Munsters, was the mixing engineer. Lee, who was drinking a lot of Scotch at the time, told Tony that Ronnie and Vinny would sneak back into the studio later in the evening after everyone had left. Lee then claimed that Ronnie would raise the volume on the vocals and drum tracks. When Tony confronted Ronnie with the accusations, he denied them and would continue to do so for the rest of his life.

"We hit the roof," said Tony, "and we had a big blow-up in the studio."[67] During the argument, Geezer also accused Ronnie and Vinny of working on a solo project during the album's mixing without telling the other members of the band.

There were other issues as well. Tony felt that Ronnie had started to get a little too bossy.

"Ronnie had started to take over a little bit too much and was becoming a bit of a Hitler," said Tony "We were working on the *Live Evil* record in Los Angeles, and in fact we nicknamed him 'Little Hitler.'"

---

[67] Ironman, My Journey Through Heaven and Hell with Black Sabbath, by Tony Iommi with T.J. Lammers, Da Capo Press, 2011.

Geezer described the *Live Evil* mixing sessions as, "The Yanks against the Brits," adding, "I think Ronnie seemed to desperately want to do his own stuff and we sort of wanted to keep it going as it was."

"Ronnie wanted more say in things," said Tony. "And Geezer would get upset with him and that is where the rot set in. *Live Evil* is when it all fell apart. Ronnie wanted to do more of his own thing, and the engineer we were using at the time in the studio didn't know what to do, because Ronnie was telling him one thing and we were telling him another. At the end of the day, we just said, 'That's it, the band is over.'"[68]

Infuriated over the charges, Ronnie quit the band with Vinny, his fellow exile, close behind. It would take years, but eventually Tony would concede that the accusations by De Carlo may have been wrong.

Following Ronnie's exit, Tony and Geezer went ahead and finished producing the *Live Evil* record which was released in December of 1982. Ronnie, who wasn't happy with the album, said, "I refuse to listen to *Live Evil* because there are too many problems. If you look at the credits, the vocals and drums are listed off to the side. Open up the album and see how many pictures there are of Tony, and how many there are of me and Vinny."[69]

- Ronnie James Dio left Black Sabbath in October of 1982, but despite the bitter break-up, Ronnie would say years later that being in Black Sabbath was one of the happiest experiences of his life. Sabbath allowed him the creative freedom to write "as dark and doomy, and gloomy, and as evil as I wanted to."[70]

As for Ronnie, a new chapter in his life was about to be written and the best was yet to come.

---

[68] Wikipedia, Black Sabbath.
[69] Wikipedia, *Live Evil*.
[70] Interview with Tony Blair, 1997.

Chapter Six
Dio

Ronnie's abrupt split from Black Sabbath was unexpected and left his fans stunned and wondering what he was going to do. It wouldn't take long however for the resourceful vocalist to form his own band.

Unshackled from the constraints of Sabbath, and feeling that he had paid his dues, Ronnie was poised to begin a new career. It was now his turn to call all the shots and create whatever music he desired.

Speaking about the time, Vinny Appice said, "Dio had no clear direction for the band when he formed it in 1982, and he'd expected to stay with Black Sabbath instead. Ronnie had a solo deal while he was in Black Sabbath. His first plan was to stay with Black Sabbath and do a solo record with all his friends on it. He wanted me to play on it, Cozy Powell, all his friends in different bands. It would be like an all-star album."

"Then things soured up with Sabbath. Things got a little bit funky, and he decided, that's it, he's leaving. Then it became, he's going to use that record deal to launch a new career. That's when he asked me if I wanted to join, and I said 'Yeah. Fuck yeah!' I was just a kid, but Ronnie was a great leader. I looked at him as a brother. I loved Tony and Geezer too. They asked me to stay, but it was just a lot easier to go with Ronnie and start something new."[71]

When asked if Ronnie was prepared for the incredible solo career that was to come, the drummer replied, "To tell you the truth, I don't think so. He might have had a vision of what he wanted. But it never was planned out, what the band should sound like. The band created its own sound."[72]

---

[71] *Teamrock.com*, July 23, 2016, by Martin Kielty.
[72] Ibid.

For a time, before putting a band together, Ronnie and Vinny rehearsed in a small wooden shed in the back of Ronnie's house, with Ronnie on bass and Vinny on the skins. "He sat on a stool and he sang," said Appice. "We had 'Holy Diver' riffs floating around and a couple of other riffs. And we'd record it on cassette."[73]

It was around this time that Ronnie's attention turned to forming a suitable band. The first thing he had to do was find a great guitar player. Jake E. Lee, the guitar wiz in Rough Cutt was auditioned, but Ronnie decided he wanted a European guitarist. Having played with both Americans and Europeans, Ronnie found that he preferred the style of the European players. He felt that they were more about heart and soul and less about being slick and flashy, like their American counterparts.

Knowing there was only one place to find the right axeman, Ronnie and Vinny flew to London where they had arranged to meet up with Ronnie's old band mate Jimmy Bain. Having been contacted by Ronnie, Jimmy said he knew several guitar players and would have them audition as soon as he got off the road. Arriving in London, "It was the first time I roomed with Ronnie," said Vinny. "Ronnie likes to read… a lot; through the night he could read a whole book. I'm trying to sleep and telling him to turn off the lights."

While waiting for Jimmy, Ronnie and Vinny had a few days to scout for guitarists. The two musicians looked through the Melody Maker paper and found that there were several local bands performing in the area. The first stop on their scouting mission was the famous Marquee Club in London, where Motörhead was playing. The place was jam-packed and incredibly loud. Pinned up against a wall Ronnie and Vinny watched wide-eyed as Motörhead tore through their set at full throttle. The next night the pair ended up at a reggae

---

[73] *TeamRock.com*, Dio: The Acrimonious Story Behind Holy Diver, July 10, 2016, by Mick Wall.

show, but had no luck finding a guitarist. "We went in and everyone was a Rasta, except us," said Ronnie. "Wrong place for us, good pint though." The following day, Jimmy returned from the road and the trio finally got together.

For the next few days Ronnie tried out a number of guitarists, but to no avail. Running low on six-string contenders, Jimmy played recordings of two guitarists that he knew of, John Sykes and Vivian Campbell. Both were great, but Ronnie decided he like Vivian's playing just a little better. Jimmy then explained that he had seen Vivian play in the band Sweet Savage, when they opened for Jimmy's band Wild Horses in Ireland.

Campbell, who was born in Northern Ireland, joined Sweet Savage when he was just 15-years-old. Vivian's wizardry on the guitar, even at such a young age, helped make Sweet Savage a predominant part of a movement coined "The New Wave of British Heavy Metal." The movement began in the United Kingdom during the 1970s and achieved international attention by the early 1980s. Iron Maiden, Motörhead, Saxon and Def Leppard were the most notable acts produced during the time. Although considered a pioneer of the NWOBHM movement, Sweet Savage never achieved commercial fame and split up in 1982.

After some discussion, Ronnie agreed that they should audition Vivian, but unfortunately the young guitarist lived in Ireland and Jimmy didn't have his phone number. This didn't stop Jimmy. Having been drinking most of the night, he thought nothing of calling the directory in Northern Ireland and asking to speak to Vivian Campbell near Belfast. Over at the Campbell residence the phone rang at 2 o'clock in the morning, waking up Vivian's father, who was also named Vivian.

None too happy about the late night caller, Vivian Sr. woke his son up telling him that, "There's a drunken Scotsman on the phone."[74]

Handing the phone to his son, Vivian was surprised when he found that it was Jimmy Bain, the bass player for Wild Horses. He and Jimmy had only met one time before. Jimmy explained that he was with Ronnie Dio and Vinny Appice in a hotel room in London. He wanted to know if Vivian could fly to London tomorrow and audition for a band Ronnie was putting together. The news was exciting, but, at the time the 19-year-old musician was broke and still living at home. Luckily, Vivian's dad was a strong supporter of his son's musical ambitions and agreed to lend his son the money for a plane ticket.

The next day, with his Les Paul in hand, Vivian boarded a plane to London. Once there he rented a Marshall amp and together with Ronnie, Jimmy and Vinny headed to John Hennery's studio in North London.

At the studio, Ronnie picked up one of Jimmy's bass guitars and showed Vivian the riff and arrangement of a song he had been working on called "Holy Diver." The two played the song over and over. Taking a break, Ronnie told Vivian to keep playing while he rolled some joints. When Vivian came to the solo part the young guitar player kept playing. As every guitarist does, Vivian had a repertoire of flashy little licks and tricks that he went through. After exhausting his impressive catalog, the young prodigy began to ad lib.

"I had to rely on instinct and I started to play basic Chuck Berry rock 'n' roll licks," said Vivian. "I was playing off of feel and baring my soul."[75]

---

[74] Vivian Campbell interview with James Curl, December 14, 2016.
[75] Ibid.

As Vivian played, Ronnie watched with great interest. Being less concerned about technique and more about feel and imagination, he liked what he was seeing.

At the time, Ronnie was recording the entire session on tape. A few years later when Ronnie played the cassette for Vivian, and got to the point where Vivian was improvising, Ronnie excitedly pointed and exclaimed, "That's it! That's when I knew you were the guitar player for me!"

After the jam session, Ronnie was super excited and knew that he had found the right guy. In addition, because Jimmy Bain meshed so well with the band he was hired on the spot.

"Everyone in the band knew that there was instant chemistry that first day in John Henry's studio," said Vivian. "There was no working into it, there was no thinking that this was something that might come together; it was absolutely fucking stunning from the first time we played together. I think we all felt that, and I think Ronnie especially felt that."[76]

As Ronnie and his new band mates sat talking in the studio, Ronnie explained that he wanted them "to be a band and a creative unit." He then made them a promise that each member would work for a wage, and if the band was successful, by the third album everyone would receive equal compensation.

"Ronnie looked us in the eyes, shook our hands and gave us a promise," said Campbell. "In return we gave our hearts and our souls to that band."[77]

After hiring Vivian and Jimmy, Ronnie and Vinny headed back to the States. Vivian followed a few weeks later and for a time lived with Ronnie and Wendy. Having made no money playing with Rainbow, Ronnie had made out a little better in the finance department after his stint with Black Sabbath. And although he was

---

[76] Ibid.
[77] Ibid.

not a wealthy man at the time, he and Wendy had bought a modest, single-story house in the Tarzana area of Los Angeles, which they shared with a couple of dogs and cats.

From the beginning, Ronnie and Vivian's relationship was complicated. "Ronnie and I never had a great relationship personally," said Vivian. "At times we did, but it was a bit like being in a band with your dad, to be honest, because he was that much older than me. When I started, I was a kid. To correct that, it was like being in a band with your stepfather. We had this very strange kind of relationship. And I was very respectful, but also very fearful of him, because he was a hero to me."

"I was listening to *Mob Rules* and *Heaven and Hell* literally the week before I flew to London to audition for this band. So, it was a very surreal experience to be with Ronnie, and I actually lived in the house with him for many, many months too. We had a difficult kind of relationship, but it definitely worked musically. Absolutely."[78]

Once Jimmy Bain arrived, Ronnie set Vivian and Jimmy up in a cheap two-bedroom apartment in the industrial, lower class area of Oakwood, and paid the rent for them.

Finding himself in a strange city with no friends, the 20-year-old Vivian was understandably homesick and lonely. Rooming with Jimmy, who was a seasoned rocker and 14-years-older didn't help the young guitarist.

"He used to bring people back to the apartment," said Campbell. "They'd be freebasing on the kitchen table. I'd never seen anyone do cocaine, let alone melt it on a spoon over a can. I used to lock myself in my room. I'd get up in the morning and there'd be strangers laying around, wasted off their fucking tits."[79]

---

[78] *Metal Wani.com*
[79] TeamRock.com, Dio: The Acrimonious Story Behind Holy Diver, July 10, 2016, by Mick Wall.

Over in Sound Studio, work on the new album progressed. The band would rehearse in one room and then wheel their equipment across the parking lot to an adjacent building and record. Besides "Holy Diver" and the partially constructed "Don't Talk to Strangers" the rest of the songs were a conglomeration of different riffs and melodies brought to the table by Campbell and Jimmy. From there they were worked over with the help of Ronnie and Vinny. One such song was "Stand Up and Shout." "That was a Jimmy riff," says Campbell, "although he and I go back and forth on this because it was similar to an old Sweet Savage thing. But that was stolen from a Gary Moore riff, so it was six degrees of separation."[80]

The song "Rainbow in the Dark" was another cooperative effort. "We played it for Ronnie and he immediately started singing the melody on top of it," says Campbell. "And then Jimmy went over to this little Yamaha and came up with the keyboard motif. We had the fucking song written in ten minutes."[81]

The song "Invisible" was also a mutual effort, albeit accidentally. "We had one of the riffs," recalls Vinny. "Then the next night we came in, we smoked a whole bunch of pot and our soundman put the tape in backwards. It started playing, and we all sat there laughing, going, 'You asshole!' But then we started saying, 'Wait a minute, that sounds good!' So we wound up learning the riff backwards. And that's the other part of "Invisible." It's the riff forwards and the riffs backwards."[82]

"Caught in the Middle," was a song inspired by and written about Angelo Arcuri, the sound engineer who worked on several of Dio's albums, including *Holy Diver*. Angelo's life always seemed to be that of

---

[80] Ibid.
[81] Ibid.
[82] Ibid.

someone "caught in the middle of some kind of turmoil," said Ronnie.[83]

Composing the album wasn't entirely stress-free. "There was always a bit more tension in the room when Ronnie came to rehearsal," said Campbell. "He was the boss. He'd bring the wages in every week and count it out for us in cash, then keep us rehearsing to the early hours of the morning, knowing we'd be in a hurry to go out to a club and spend it."[84]

Finally on May 23, 1983 Dio released their much anticipated debut album *Holy Diver*, and it couldn't have hit the record stores at a better time. Young fans, enamored with the popular role-playing game Dungeons & Dragons and a resurgence of J.R.R Tolkien's "Hobbit" books, embraced the album's fantasy-driven lyrics and cover art. Dio added to this by releasing a video for "Holy Diver" on MTV, which at the time was two-years-old and just entering the peak of its popularity. In the video, Ronnie plays a fur-clad, sword-wielding barbarian adventuring through an abandoned church. During his journey, he encounters strange creatures and an adversary armed with a battle axe that he strikes down with his great sword.

Randy Barrett's cover art illustration also helped build on the fantasy theme by introducing Murray, the band's demon-like mascot who is apparently drowning a priest with a whirling length of chain. The shocking image of a horned demon with blazing red eyes drowning a priest was just the kind of thing young fans loved and their parents loathed.

The cover art caused a lot of controversy with religious groups who quickly dubbed the album as "satanic." Ronnie, however, would argue that appearances can be deceiving and maybe the cover really depicted a priest drowning a devil.

---

[83] You tube interview, Dio talks about *Holy Diver* songs.
[84] TeamRock.com, Dio: The Acrimonious Story Behind Holy Diver, July 10, 2016, by Mick Wall.

From the album came two massive hit singles that rocked the very core of heavy metal, "Rainbow in the Dark" and "Holy Diver." Both songs quickly found a home on MTV and got plenty of air time on the radio as well. Moreover, "Rainbow in the Dark" may well be the biggest hit Dio ever had.

At first Ronnie didn't like the song and thought it was to "poppy." In fact, he had nearly taken a razor blade to the tape and destroyed it before the rest of the guys hastily talked him out of it; something Ronnie was very grateful for when the song hit big.

There is little doubt that *Holy Diver* is the highlight of Dio's "solo" career and to this day it remains a titan among hard rock and heavy metal albums.

Canadian reviewer Martin Popoff describes the album as, "quintessential traditional metal," with Ronnie James Dio "almost single-handedly reinventing gothic hard rock for the '80s, incorporating strong melodic hooks and more than the genre's usual share of velvety, classical-based pyrotechnics."[85]

Following the release of *Holy Diver*, Wendy began scheduling shows. Not having a ton of money at the time, Ronnie mortgaged his house to come up with the funds to finance an extensive tour and stage set. "It was a big risk," said Wendy Dio, "but I believed in him. He believed in himself."[86]

It was at this time that Ronnie decided he needed a keyboard player. Up to this point Jimmy had been doing the job in addition to playing bass, but he really wasn't a proper keyboardist. So Ronnie decided to make a call.

Across town keyboardist Claude Schnell was sitting in his apartment pondering his future. Having just walked away from the band Hughes/Thrall after a year-

---

[85] *Popoff, Martin (1 November 2005). The Collector's Guide to Heavy Metal: Volume 2: The Eighties. Burlington, Ontario, Canada: Collector's Guide Publishing. ISBN 978-1-894959-31-5.*
[86] TeamRock.com, Dio: The Acrimonious Story Behind Holy Diver, July 10, 2016, by Mick Wall.

and-a-half, he was dejected and wondering what he was going to do.

A few years earlier, in late December of '79, Claude had made the long trek from Buffalo, New York to Los Angeles with his best friend Joey Cristofanilli; both were only 20-years-old. The two ambitious musicians had heard that the popularity of hard rock was exploding in Los Angeles and it was the place to be if you were looking to become a rock star.

Arriving on the Sunset Strip, they found that the stories were true. The strip was super-charged with activity and there were a lot of great bands. At night the streets came live with neon lights and the bustle of thousands of people. Long-haired rockers in concert t-shirts and curvy groupies in fishnet stockings and miniskirts were everywhere. Live music blared loudly from a multitude of smoky bars, mixing with the sounds of the city's vibrant night life.

"When you went out at night you couldn't walk down the strip without running into people," said Joey Cristofanilli. "It was like being in New York City. And the clubs were packed; it was just crazy."[87]

Well known nightclubs like The Whisky a Go Go, The Troubadour and The Roxy had lines that snaked around the block. Bands like Ratt, Dokken, Poison, Great White, Quiet Riot, W.A.S.P. and Mötley Crüe were jockeying for position and had yet to get their names on a major record label. In just a couple of years these same bands would usher in the "hair metal" era. They would rule the 1980s, MTV and the airways for a decade and create some of the most iconic music of a generation.

Excited with the undeniable opportunities the city had to offer, Claude and Joe had a band called Magic put together in no time. But it was short-lived. The two friends rebounded quickly and formed Rough Cutt, with

---

[87] Joey Cristofanilli interview with James Curl.

vocalist Paul Shortino, drummer Dave Alford and guitarist Jake E. Lee.

By 1982 the boys had made a name for themselves on the Strip and had a respectable following of die-hard fans. It was at this time that word got around that Ronnie and Wendy Dio were looking for bands to manage. Claude and Joe had heard that there was a party coming up and that Ronnie would be there.

With demo tape in hand the two friends finagled their way into the party by way of a well-connected roadie named Huey, who worked for Rod Stewart. Eventually the pair were introduced to Ronnie and Wendy and handed them the demo. With a promise to give it a listen, Ronnie took the tape. "I was just blown away," said Joey; "he was just such a gentleman."[88]

A month later the band got a call and was offered a deal to sign with Ronnie and Wendy's management group, Niji Entertainment. (The word Niji meaning rainbow in Japanese).

Right from the start Ronnie and Wendy were enthusiastic and supportive of their new band. "They opened their home to us," said Joey. "They fed us, they clothed us, they let us use their cars and they helped us with rent. I have nothing but respect for both of them. Wendy was very protective of us, we were young and she looked out for us all. Ronnie brought in a massive PA system for us and he would come down to rehearsal. He would come in, sit in the back and listen. And he wouldn't come forward until there was something he thought we needed help with; he was very constructive. And to be able to learn to craft a song from him was just such an opportunity; it was great."[89]

As talented as the original lineup of Rough Cutt was, it didn't last long or achieve great success. Jake E. Lee left and went to have a quarrelsome stint with Ozzy

---

[88] Ibid.
[89] Ibid.

Osbourne, Joey went to play for Ratt, and Claude found a spot in Hughes/Thrall. Rough Cutt was eventually repopulated and would go on tour as the opener for Dio and release a couple of moderately successful albums in the mid-1980s.

Meanwhile, back at his apartment, Claude was brooding and feeling like he had just wasted a year-and-a-half when suddenly the phone rang; much to his surprise it was Ronnie James Dio.

"Hi, Claude, it's Ronnie, how ya doing? How are things going with Glenn?" Claude explained to Ronnie that things were not well and that he had just split from the band.

"Well, I'm sorry to hear that," said Ronnie. "But, I may have a solution for you. We decided we're going to need a keyboard player to go on tour. I want you to know right up front you're going to be off-stage. I don't know how the credits are going to work; we can work that out later. But if you want to do it I'm not going to audition anyone else."[90]

Happy with the offer, Claude was nevertheless curious as to why Ronnie was offering the job without holding an audition. When Claude queried Ronnie about it, the singer said, "If you're good enough for Glenn, you're good enough for me."[91] With that being said, Claude didn't need any time to think it over; his answer was immediate—"Yeah, sure I'll do it."

The offer from Ronnie was welcome news for the keyboardist, who just moments before was wondering how long the unemployment line was going to be.

Excited with the prospects of his new band, Claude began rehearsals a few days later. On one occasion he broke down on the way to the studio in his 1974 Pantera—like most exotic cars it could be a little finicky. After making the necessary adjustments to one of the

---

[90] Claude Schnell interview with James Curl.
[91] Ibid.

Weber carburetors, he got the car back on the road and eventually made it to the studio. Arriving late, he found that Ronnie was upset. Claude knew that Ronnie wanted everyone to be on time. He also knew that Ronnie was the first one at the studio and the last one to leave and always gave 100%; he expected the same from his band mates.

After rehearsal, Ronnie wanted to see the car that Claude had been talking about. The keyboardist was only too happy to show off his prized possession. Being a true "gear head" Claude had upgraded the car to GT-5 specs and built the motor to a heart-pounding 600 hp. After looking the car over, the two decided to go for a ride.

Once on the freeway Claude unleashed the horsepower much to Ronnie's delight. On the way back, they cruised down Hollywood Boulevard, but as they neared the studio the car suddenly began to run rough and died. Getting out, Claude told Ronnie to steer while he pushed. What could only be described as a comedic scene, Ronnie got into the driver's seat. Because of his short height and the car's extremely low seats he was barely able to see over the steering wheel. With Claude huffing and puffing and Ronnie doing his best to steer, Claude pushed the Pantera into a gas station parking lot.

Speaking of the incident the keyboardist said he was grateful there were no cell phones at the time. "Can you imagine that happening now?" said Claude. "Someone would have recorded us on their cell phone and put it on You Tube."[92]

With Claude seated firmly at the keyboards, albeit behind the curtains, Dio took off on the *Holy Diver* world tour. Their first stop was at the Concert Barn in Antioch, California on July 23, 1983 and it was nothing fancy. The large, dirt floor barn, once used to store cattle and livestock had been converted into a concert hall. Resting on several acres of pasture land in the middle of nowhere

---

[92] Claude Schnell interview with James Curl.

it was difficult for fans to find. As a result, Ronnie and Wendy along with some of the band members answered quite a few phone calls from concert-goers looking for directions. When not on the phone, the band prepared for the show and barbequed with the owner, Bob Ginocchio.

Being their first show, Ronnie was only expecting a modest turnout of a few hundred. But, by the time he and his band mates hit the stage they were floored to find that over 3,000 fans had crammed themselves into the big barn. The unexpected turnout broke all previous attendance records.

Despite the dirt floors, rustic accommodations and questionable acoustics, fans were treated to an unforgettable night of rock 'n' roll, first with Rough Cutt then with Dio. "I remember it like it was yesterday," said metal fan Daniel Smith. "Showed up early to get up front. We drove up in a red '67 Mustang with my brother David and our friend Cindy Crosby. It was a magical time."[93]

"Saw this Dio show while standing on the dirt floor," said another attendee Lewis Greg. "Finding that place was a major pain and we almost gave up. This was the only show I saw at the Concert Barn and while the energy was good from the bands, the sound/acoustics were horrible, to say the least. But being Dio's first solo show, it was historic."[94]

Speaking of the first show, Vivian Campbell said, "I'll never forget it. Jimmy came over during 'Invisible' and went to lean on me right as I turned away, and he fell off the stage. He didn't miss a beat. He was down but not out."[95]

Years later Ronnie recalled Dio's first gig, saying, "We had just started, first album *Holy Diver*. Someone

---

[93] *Adventureamegios.net:* Let's go back in time to Antioch, a barn and Dio, September 20, 2013.
[94] Ibid.
[95] *TeamRock.com*, Dio: The Acrimonious Story Behind Holy Diver, July 10, 2016, by Mick Wall.

said, 'You're playing the Concert Barn in Antioch.' We drove out there in a bus. The bus took us there. We kept driving and driving, took a left and we went past nothing. We took a right and went past more nothing and then left. I went, 'This is a joke.' Remember, I had played with Sabbath and we had played for hundreds of thousands of people. I went, 'Is this what my life has come to?' We turned up at that place and there weren't that many people there because we got there really early in the day. We went to the house that was there and they made food. It was great."

"Then we went to the dressing area which was a trailer of some kind behind the stage. The next thing I know, we're up onstage and there are 3,000 people in the place. Suddenly, we had broken every record that Antioch ever had and every record that Antioch ever will have and it was magnificent. That was the first time that we'd ever played. The only material that we knew was all of *Holy Diver* which we did and some Sabbath songs and some Rainbow songs. Luckily, we had those too. I will never forget it. It was one of the most defining career moments of my life."[96]

From Antioch, Dio hit the road and played ten shows as the opening act for Aerosmith, which didn't make Ronnie particularly happy. Following a fist fight on stage between Steven Tyler and Joe Perry, Ronnie decided to head out on his own, this time with Queensrÿche as the warm-up act.

By August the band was in Europe playing at the Monsters of Rock at Castle Donington. Back in the States a month later, Ronnie and the boys blazed a trail across America that left their fans hoarse and wanting more. The tour finally concluded on January 7, 1984 at the Arlington theatre before a sold-out crowd of raucous headbangers.

---

[96] *Kaos2000* Magazine interview, Ronnie James Dio, March 27, 2000, by Philip Anderson and Joe Camareno.

Wanting to continue their momentum, the band took a short break then immediately began working on the follow-up to *Holy Diver*. For the new record, Ronnie decided to get away from L.A. and relocate to Colorado's Caribou Ranch recording studio. "Once we wrote the title track 'The Last in Line,'" said Vivian, "we were confident we had our centerpiece for the record, so Ronnie booked Caribou Ranch."

Sandy Tomes, one if the directors at the ranch who dealt first-hand with the various bands, fondly remembers Dio's arrival saying, "Dio was a question mark; when they came it was sort of out of our norm. The first project I ever did at the ranch was Amy Grant. So they were coming and we were all kinda like, 'Well, I wonder what this is going to be like.' Dio came in and right away they just endeared themselves to everyone. We loved them and they loved us. And we had a really good time."[97]

Located near Nederland, Colorado in the Rocky Mountains, the Caribou studio was a state of the art facility that hosted over 150 big name artists in its heyday, including Michael Jackson, Elton John, Frank Zappa, Joe Walsh and the Beach Boys, to name a few. The open spaces, fresh air and beautiful mountain scenery inspired Joe Walsh to write the hit song "Rocky Mountain Way."

The facility was like a small self-contained city nestled at the foot of the Rocky Mountains. The main building was a large barn that had been converted into a recording studio in the early 1970s. Sprawled out near the studio were over a half-dozen rustic cabins that housed the various artists and their entourages. Each of the cabins had an Indian name such as Chipeta, Wigwam and Running Bear. The largest cabin was Ouray and it was the one Ronnie stayed in.

---

[97] Sandy Tomes interview with James Curl.

The place boasted all the amenities one would expect to accommodate such high-end clientele, such as recreational rooms with pool tables and dart boards as well as a mess hall and a 24-hour on-call chef. Large two-sided fireplaces warmed the lavishly decorated rooms, something Ronnie and his band mates were thankful for since recording took place during the frigid winter months. "There was a lot of snow, like four feet," said Vivian. "We had to carve out pathways to walk from one building to another."[98]

The chef was put to good use at least one time when Ronnie requested Braciole, an Italian dish consisting of thin, pan-fried meat stuffed with cheese and served smothered in a zesty tomato sauce. Not familiar with the Italian cuisine, the chef was unable to prepare it. This didn't, however, stop Ronnie's resourceful keyboardist, Claude. A quick call to his former band mate Joey Cristofanilli and Claude was in touch with Joey's mom Mary, who was known to be an outstanding cook. She gave the chef the recipe and instructed him on how to make the meal. A while later dinner was served and it was just as Ronnie liked it.

Secluded away from the outside world, the band created unperturbed. Typical recording sessions started at around 11:00 a.m. and ran until well after midnight, with some sessions going until the early morning hours.

"It was great," said Vivian, "because we got to focus on making the record; there were no distractions and such."[99]

While the seclusion was conducive for the creation of the album, some found the quiet isolation difficult to handle. "When everyone got stir-crazy at the ranch," said Sandy, "they would head down to the Pioneer Inn for some drinks. I had a tequila shot contest with Jimmy Bain. I won, but I think he let me win."

---

[98] Vivian Campbell interview with James Curl.
[99] Ibid.

Jimmy in particular found the solitude unnerving. "I know Ronnie got pissed at Jimmy," said Vivian, "because Jimmy was such a social person that he couldn't stand it that it was so isolated. So he took a car down to Boulder which was the closest city. It was a Friday night and he went down to see the Scorpions play. And he came back with a bunch of strangers and Ronnie got mad. But that was typical Jimmy, ya know. Jimmy was such a social animal, he needed that sort of energy of a party atmosphere around him. That's what he thrived off of."[100]

With Ronnie and the boys hard at work, fans eagerly anticipated the next Dio arrival. Expectations were understandably high; would the new album live up to the immensely popular *Holy Diver*?

On July 2, 1984 impatient fans got what they had been waiting for and they were not disappointed. With Murray, the band's demonic mascot once again dominating the cover art, *The Last in Line* was planted firmly in the realm of sword and sorcery fantasy, something Dio fans had come to embrace.

Introducing songs like, "Mystery," "Egypt," "Evil Eyes" and "The Last in Line," lyrically the album expressed a strong feeling of the medieval. Listening to Ronnie's poetic vocals and the band's classical melodies, it's easy for the listener to become lost in a reverie of make believe. Adding to this came videos on MTV for the hit singles "The Last in Line" and "Mystery." Both were fantasy-based and featured wizards, fairies and otherworldly creatures. In "The Last in Line" video, Ronnie is garbed as an ancient Egyptian.

At the local record stores, hordes of metal fans were clearing out the shelves as fast as they were stocked, and by September the album was certified gold with over 500,000 copies sold. The excited fans were eager to get the record home and onto their turntables, or cassette

---

[100] Ibid.

tapes into the decks of their 1960s and '70s muscle cars. What a glorious time in America!

Although most felt that the album had not quite reached the stellar height of *Holy Diver*, *The Last in Line* was nevertheless a worthy follow-up, and to this day is considered a genuinely great album.

By the time Dio headed out on *The Last in Line* tour in 1984 the band had become extremely successful and its popularity had increased exponentially. The ensuing tour reflected Dio's rise in fame and the overall popularity of heavy metal, which was by now at the peak of its headbanging powers. The band was selling out huge arenas like the Forum in Los Angeles and Madison Square Garden in New York. These venues seated over 15,000 respectively and were filled to capacity with swarms of screaming metal fans. All across Europe, Japan and Australia the same story held true.

With the massively successful *The Last in Line* tour wrapped up in January of 1985, Ronnie and his band mates took a well-deserved breather. Writing for a new album commenced a few months later, but there was a growing resentment and a grumbling among some of the members. Trouble was right around the corner.

Chapter Seven
Vivian Exits

It was during the writing process of *Sacred Heart* that the first signs of serious trouble within the band started to surface. Vivian had begun questioning Ronnie about their original financial agreement. The young guitarist wanted Ronnie to honor a commitment he'd made about everyone getting an equal share of the money, but Ronnie kept putting it off. Every time Viv would bring it up, Ronnie's retort was they would talk about it later. As a result, their relationship became strained and Vivian began to slowly withdraw and lose interest.

In addition to this, Ronnie's marriage to Wendy was crumbling and nearing the final stages of its collapse. The two were separated and going through an emotionally turbulent time, often resulting in loud, volatile screaming matches. This was nothing new; their marriage had been unstable and for years and had consistently been an on again/off again love affair, but this time it was ending for good.

"Ronnie was in a really, really dark place by the time we were writing the *Sacred Heart* record," said Campbell, "and his mood reflected it. That record never felt as good as *Holy Diver* or *The Last in Line*. And it was painful to make for a lot of reasons, and I think it transmits into the music. Ronnie's mood was really dark."[101]

Continuing, Vivian said, "When we were making *Holy Diver* and *The Last in Line* we were there 24/7 and we gave 100%. We were there encouraging each other, nobody left the studio early and everyone was encouraging everyone else. We were a team and that's

---

[101] Vivian Campbell interview with James Curl.

why those early records are so great. Things started to change by the *Sacred Heart* record. By the time we got to *Sacred Heart* everyone left the studio as soon as they could. You did your parts and you left. Ronnie was really hard work to be around for that record; his separation from Wendy really affected him and had a major impact."[102]

As tension in the band slowly built, work progressed on *Sacred Heart*. It was during this time that Viv and Jimmy attended a 48-hour radiothon called Rock Relief for Africa put on by the L.A. station 95.5 KLOS. During the event, Campbell and Jimmy realized that participation from the heavy metal community was practically non-existent. It didn't take long however for the imaginative pair to come up with an idea to write a song geared around the heavy metal genre. The song would generate money and awareness for famine relief in Africa.

"We're doing the interview," said Campbell, "and it was at the time that 'We Are the World,' that Michael Jackson project, had come out. The DJ said to us, 'How come no one, absolutely no one, in the rock community was invited to participate in this?' And you know, when you think about it, back in that era hard rock music sold millions of records but it didn't have any sort of respect in the music industry. It never won Grammys or anything. It was always kind of frowned upon."

"So, we kind of had a bit of conversation on air with the DJ about that and we kind of jokingly said that we should do our own thing, and Jimmy came up with the name right there and then and said, 'We should call it Hear 'n Aid.' We all kind of fell off our stools laughing about that and at the time Jimmy and I lived together; we were roommates during those early Dio records. We

---

[102] Ibid.

went back to our apartment later that night and you know, we said, hey, let's give it some serious consideration. Let's actually look into the possibilities of doing this. We wrote the song that night."[103]

Jimmy and Vivian knew that the idea was an incredibly ambitious venture. They also knew that they couldn't accomplish the project without a strong leader, so they approached Ronnie with the idea. Initially, Ronnie was cold toward the proposal and showed little interested in getting involved. "He wasn't on board with it at first," said Campbell. "He wasn't against the idea, but we just had so much going on. Like I said he was producing the record and he was also writing all the lyrics for *Sacred Heart*. I think he felt overwhelmed."[104]

Eventually, after weeks of pestering by Viv and Jimmy, Ronnie agreed to discuss the idea with Wendy, who was, despite their marriage woes, still his manager. Finally, after some consideration they agreed to get involved.

"Initially, I didn't really want to take part in the project," said Ronnie. "I was busy doing our own album which was *Sacred Heart* and I felt that it was just another one of those projects, another problem to deal with."[105] However, after becoming educated about the widespread famine in Africa, and previous projects like Band Aid that had been done to raise money and awareness, Ronnie's attitude changed and he became completely caught up in the project.

"It made me realize," said Dio, "what an awful person I must have been not to have realized that this is an

---

[103] Ibid.
[104] *Shutupandrockon.com,* interview with Vivian Campbell, March 4, 2017.
[105] YouTube interview.

ongoing problem." With Ronnie taking up the leadership role of captain, Hear 'n Aid quickly built up steam.

Like other charity songs, the idea was to gather a supergroup of musicians, in this case hard rock's biggest stars, and have everyone participate in a song. Ronnie knew that this was ground-breaking and something that had never been attempted, let alone accomplished within the annals of hard rock. The singer also knew that the project presented a number of formidable challenges, but Ronnie was never one to balk when things got tough.

The first, and perhaps biggest challenge, was to get in touch with as many big-name rockers as possible and get them to agree to help. With a course of action laid out, Vivian and Jimmy, along with Wendy, began the arduous task of reaching out to some of metal's most notable "stars." This took weeks of tedious phone calls to managers and agents but eventually yielded great results—40 of rock's biggest A-listers answered the call and agreed to contribute.

"I spent literally weeks and weeks making phone calls to people," said Vivian. "Just 'hi, you don't know me but I'm Vivian Campbell, I play guitar for Dio,' and gave them the whole spiel about this is what we're doing and is there any way you can participate? We pulled it off, it was incredibly hard work. But you know, I don't think we would have been able to do it without Ronnie lending his support."[106]

"Hear 'n Aid had to be a non-profit organization," said Wendy. "We had to set up a board of directors, 14 people, and all decisions had to be made by the board. My role was getting the licensing. The musicians were fantastic, they'll always give their right arm and leg for charity, but then you have to get permissions from their

---

[106] *Shutupandrockon.com,* interview with Vivian Campbell, March 4, 2017.

managers and record companies. That was a nightmare. It dragged on for months after the track was completed."[107]

While the group was being gathered, the first thing Ronnie did was write the lyrics for the music Viv and Jimmy had composed. He came up with a song titled "Stars." Lyrically, the track is very Dio-esque and as was his modus operandi, included lines about rainbows and magic.

With the lyrics completed, he then tasked Claude "with recording all the vocal melody lines on piano, so that said melodies could be distributed in advance to all the singers involved. This way they could learn their lines and melodies without being influenced by hearing them being sung by a proper singer. Very clever idea by Ronnie and, evidently, it worked like a charm."[108]

Claude was also responsible for composing and recording all of the extended piano music which plays over the credits at the end of the documentary video.

On May 20th long limousines and luxury sedans began dropping off rock stars at A&M Records Studios in Hollywood for a two-day recording session. To add a little comedy relief, Michael McKean and Harry Shearer, better known as David St. Hubbins and Derek Smalls of the parody band Spinal Tap, were also in attendance and in character. Not only did they have everyone laughing, they were also there to lend their "mighty pipes" to the choir as well. "I've got pipes," said Davis St. Hubbins. "I've got pipes I haven't used yet."

When asked about the project and if there were any clashing of egos, Claude Schnell replied, "It was awesome from start to finish. Everyone was on their best

---

[107] The story of Hear N' Aid, the heavy metal Band Aid, May 16, 2017, by Johnny Black.
[108] Claude Schnell interview with James Curl.

behavior and all egos were left out on La Brea Avenue. It helped that Ronnie was captain of that particular ship and everyone held him in highest esteem. The whole thing had like a big, happy family picnic sort of vibe. Also, everyone knew what a ridiculously ambitious project this was for Ronnie and Angelo Arcuri and were collectively honored and curious to see how it would turn out."[109]

As one might imagine with all that wild rock star hair running around it took a talented hair stylist to tame it. After all, it was the '80s, a decade known for its big hair. To handle the job, Wendy brought in Joey Belfiore, Ronnie's personal hairdresser along with his assistant Annie.

Joey, who was not only an amazing hair stylist but also a talented drummer, had been taking care of Ronnie's hair since the early 1980s. Reflecting about how he got the job cutting Ronnie's hair, Joey said, "When I started working with Ronnie, Claude and I were living together. He came to our house because he wanted Claude to work on his new solo record *Holy Diver*. We had Randy Rhoads, Robbin Crosby, Billy Sheehan, Jake E. Lee, and Warren DeMartini, all these people over, and they were all my clients at the time. David Lee Roth and Glenn Hughes used to come over too and party and get high. They would play Claude's piano and have singing contests."

"So, Ronnie came over and he wanted Claude to listen to "Rainbow in the Dark." So that's when I got to him because he kept playing with his hair and I talked to him once before about it and he said, 'I'm very unhappy with my hair, because when I go out there my hair has to look right and I got this thing on my head.'" Ronnie then

---

[109] Ibid.

92

showed Joey the large scar he'd gotten as a result of the car wreck back in 1968 that killed Nicky Pantas.

Ronnie then explained that everyone cuts his hair wrong and thinks that he's going bald. Joey however knew that Ronnie wasn't going bald, it was just the scar.

"It just needed special attention," explained Joey. "So when I told him I could cut his hair the right way, he gave me 'one shot.' He goes, 'Okay, well my hair is my thing, and I'm gonna give you a shot.'"[110]

A few days later at Ronnie's home, Joey got his "shot." "He was real fussy," said Joey. "I remember when I first started doing it, he would use the downstairs mirror in the bathroom, go look at it, put his hands through it and then come back and say, 'Okay, can you do a little bit more? This feels kinda heavy.' You know he wanted it perfect. That's how it was at first. And then after I did it the first time I changed his whole look completely—I gave him bangs."

Joey then said, "When he ran on stage he ran around and his hair would pop up in the front and go all the way back and he didn't like that, so I cut half of it and all the crown and the bangs and I made that short, so it would push forward and have height on top and cover around his face to give him confidence. As soon as I did that it changed the way he was on stage, it gave him more confidence."[111]

Having impressed Ronnie with his hair-cutting abilities, Joey was hired and paid $200 dollars for his service. The pay was substantial considering it was the early 1980s; today that would be a $500 dollar haircut. Moreover, from that day forward Joey would remain Ronnie's hair stylist for over two decades. The two would even come up with a name for the stubborn

---

[110] Joey Belfiore interview with James Curl.
[111] Ibid.

cowlick, or swirl of hair at the back of Ronnie head that always wanted to stick up. "Ronnie named it 'Erick,'" said Joey. "When I would cut his hair he would ask, 'How's Erick doing today?'"

Over the years, Joey would make Ronnie and his hair look great for all the videos during the MTV era as well as dozens of magazine covers. The two became good friends and Joey got to know Ronnie on an intimate level to which few were privy.

"Whenever I went over to his house to do his hair," said Joey, "he would smoke and pour us a drink, Sambuca. He would put it in the microwave with a few coffee beans on top and then we would sit there and he would play some music, especially the music he was working on. And I would say that's really heavy stuff and he would say, 'Yeah, make my hair like that.' And after I got done cutting his hair he would walk me to his car and he would ask me if my car was okay, you know, just concerned about your well-being, just really cool and just a really nice man and so generous. If you treated him right, he would treat you right, right back."[112]

Back at the epic charity session, with Joey having made everyone's hair look great, the cameras rolled and recording began. The single original track for the project, "Stars," was an inspiring hard rocker that, had it been included on *Sacred Heart*, could easily have been that album's smash single. Lead vocals on the song were shared by a prestigious group of premier singers from both hard rock and heavy metal that included Rob Halford, Kevin DuBrow, Eric Bloom, Geoff Tate, Dave Meniketti, Don Dokken, Paul Shortino and of course Ronnie himself.

The three-minute guitar solo was handled by a renowned group of lightning-fingered virtuosos, with

---

[112] Ibid.

each getting a moment to display their superlative skills. The impressive gathering was without a doubt one of the finest ever assembled for any project, and was comprised of Vivian Campbell, Carlos Cavazo, Buck Dharma, Brad Gillis, Craig Goldy, George Lynch, Yngwie Malmsteen, Eddie Ojeda, and Neal Schon. Iron Maiden's Dave Murray and Adrian Smith were in the middle of their World Slavery Tour at the time, but were able to fly in and attend the main recording session as rhythm guitarists.

Recalling the unique session, Vivian said, "You put a bunch of '80s guitarists in the same room and, of course, there's going to be competition for bragging rights. They were even arguing about who had the biggest hair."

The choir consisted of Tommy Aldridge, Dave Alford, Carmine Appice, Vinny Appice, Jimmy Bain, Frankie Banali, Mick Brown, Vivian Campbell, Carlos Cavazo, Amir Derakh, Buck Dharma, Brad Gillis, Craig Goldy, Chris Hagar, Chris Holmes, Blackie Lawless, George Lynch, Yngwie Malmsteen, Mick Mars, Michael McKean, Vince Neil, Ted Nugent, Eddie Ojeda, Jeff Pilson, Rudy Sarzo, Claude Schnell, Neal Schon, Harry Shearer, Mark Stein and Matt Thorr.

Bass duties were handled by Jimmy Bain, and drums were covered by Vinny Appice and Frankie Banali.

Despite the problems of a failing marriage and a hectic workload that may have had a lesser man tossing in the towel, Ronnie held firm throughout the project and displayed incredible resolve and leadership ability. It also helped that he had Angelo Arcuri in his corner as engineer. Angelo was indispensable getting the project completed.

As producer, Ronnie was in charge and was "present in the studio from the first down beat of the backing tracks to the last fade on the final mix," said Claude Schnell. "I shudder to think of how many decision he had to make in the course of producing just that one song. Had to be in the thousands."[113]

For Ronnie it was a lot of hard work, but in the end he said it had opened his heart and was, "satisfying, extremely satisfying."[114]

Final mixing of the song "Stars" took place at Rumbo Studios in L.A. The song was then added to a compilation album that contained live tracks by Kiss, Motörhead, Dio, Accept, Rush and Scorpions, as well as studio recordings by Y&T and Jimi Hendrix.

Originally the album, along with the documentary, was slated to be released shortly after recording. However, because of contractual problems with some of the artists' record labels the release date was pushed back to January 1, 1986. The six-month delay somewhat reduced the impact of the album. Nevertheless, it went on to raise over one million dollars within the first year and over three million since then.

Having completed the Hear 'n Aid project, Ronnie refocused his attention on the *Sacred Heart* album and work resumed. A few months later, on August 15, 1985, the record was released.

Despite a lot of negativity during the composition of the album, it managed to reach #29 on the Billboard 200 chart. And although many fans felt the album lacked the inspiration of the previous two releases, it still produced several outstanding tracks, like "Sacred Heart," "Hungry for Heaven," "Rock 'n' Roll Children," and "The King of Rock 'n' Roll." Moreover, the album sold extremely well and by October it was certified gold. The pop metal song "Hungry for Heaven" was even featured in the 1985 movie *Vision Quest*, starring Matthew Modine.

---

[113] Claude Schnell interview with James Curl.
[114] You Tube video part 1 of 2, Much Music 1986 interview.

The cover art, while still fantasy-based, was a departure from the last two albums and introduced a new band mascot, called Dean the Dragon, (sometimes referred to as Denzel). Surrounding the dragon are the Latin words: "Finis per somnium reperio tibi sacra cor veneficus aurum," which translates into English as: "Come the end by sleep; I will prepare for you the Sacred Heart which is the magic that opens upon the altar."

For all its success at the record stores, many of Dio's hardcore fans were turned off by the new songwriting direction and the more commercial sound. *Sacred Heart* would be the last Dio album that would reach the lofty gold level, and marked a steady decline in album sales that the band would not recover from until the release of *Magica*, some 15-years-later.

By the time *Sacred Heart* was released, Dio was at the absolute peak of their popularity. In October of '85 they left on the first leg of a marathon world tour that would see them play over a hundred shows and spend a total of 14 months on the road. However, there were serious problems within the band. The rift between Ronnie and Vivian had worsened and was quickly starting to come to a head. Over the past several months Vivian had become a "constant thorn" in Ronnie's side. He had been constantly questioning Ronnie about their original deal that was agreed upon when he initially auditioned for the band.

"I wanted them to uphold Ronnie's end of the deal," said Viv. "In fairness to Wendy, she never knew the deal because she wasn't in the room when the deal was discussed. The deal was first brought up that night in John Henry's. I'm not sure Ronnie even remembered the deal, he was so stoned."[115]

---

[115] Vivian Campbell interview with James Curl.

"When the original Dio band went in to do the *Holy Diver* record," said Campbell, "Ronnie had written the title track and he was working on 'Don't Talk to Strangers.' And the other seven songs on the record we wrote collectively here in L.A. and the same for *The Last In Line* album and the *Sacred Heart* album—they were very, very much a band effort. And that's what Ronnie wanted, ironically. That first night when I auditioned for the band in London, that's what Ronnie told us. He said he left Black Sabbath and he had an existing solo deal. We were gonna call the band Dio—obviously, for name recognition. Nobody's gonna call it Campbell or Bain or Appice. And it made perfect sense."

"He said, 'You're gonna work on a wage, but we're gonna create together as a band.' And he said, 'If this is successful, by the third album we'll make it an equity situation.' And that's why I got fired—because I was the first one to hold my hand up and say, 'Ronnie, we've done the third album. Remember that night in London?' And he just kept pushing it off and pushing it off, and he said, 'We'll talk about it when Wendy gets here.' And in hindsight, I now realize that he never shared his initial vision with his ex-wife, Wendy, who was managing the band. And she had a whole different idea; she wanted Ronnie to be the solo artist. She didn't see the value in what Ronnie saw, in the band being a creative unit. She just didn't get that. She just thought it was Ronnie and whoever. Get a bunch of guys on stage; it doesn't matter. Well, guess what—it does matter. It makes a big difference."[116]

"The original Dio band was a four-piece creative unit and Wendy never understood that. She's not musical. So, Ronnie and I, I think would have been fine. She doesn't

---

[116] MetalWani.com

know that the sign of a great band is the sum of the parts."[117]

Realizing that the issues with Vivian were not going to go away, plans were already being made to maneuver Craig Goldy, the guitarist for Rough Cutt, into Vivian's spot.

Vivian's termination from the band came about when he returned home to Ireland for a break between the American leg of the *Sacred Heart* tour and before the start of their run through Europe. It was during this time that Vivian received a FedEx envelope from Wendy that contained a letter and a contract that offered the guitarist another $400 a week over his regular pay. The cover letter stated that failure to sign the contract would constitute immediate termination from the band.

Angered over the unexpected letter, and unwilling to sign a deal that was not part of the original agreement, Vivian immediately tried to contact Ronnie. After repeated attempts, Viv realized that Ronnie was avoiding him. A week later, as scheduled, Dio began the European portion of their tour, with Craig Goldy replacing Vivian.

"I would like to point out that I did not leave the band," said Vivian. "That myth has been perpetuated for decades. It was perpetuated by the Dio camp because it suited their agenda. So many people here 30-something years later still think that I left Dio, but it was never my intention to leave the band."[118]

"The reason I was fired from the band was that I refused to accept a contract that they offered me which was contrary to the original agreement Ronnie had made with Jimmy, Vinny and myself when the band was first formed. Wendy had different ideas for how it was going

---

[117] Vivian Campbell interview with James Curl.
[118] Ibid.

to be and for me; it was a matter of principle and I refused to sign the contract and that's why I was fired."[119]

Jimmy Bain also resented the lack of recognition he felt that he and the other members had received for their part in creating *Holy Diver*, not least from Ronnie and Wendy. As a result, he harbored deep feelings of resentment and his words resonated much of what Campbell said.

"It was supposed to be Dio's solo album for the first record," said Jimmy, "and then it was going to become a band thing where we would all make equal splits from it. And of course what happened was that the first album did so well and the band did so well on the first record that it never became discussed after that, and so it was just Ronnie and Wendy Dio and there was Viv and myself and Vinny as almost 'hired guns.' You know and it never became that band it was supposed to become."

"It started off with all the potential and all the promises and everything like that and it never materialized. We basically ended up getting shafted by the Dio people. We did the first album for $150 a week because that's all they said they could afford, but when the album went platinum you don't think they'd turn around and give us 25 or 30 thousand dollars because they made a couple million off it? We didn't get a dime more than what we'd made when we recorded the album, which was $150 a week. And they never came back and gave us anything."[120]

"I didn't join the band as a hired hand; I was under the impression we were a proper band."[121]

Jimmy also felt that getting rid of Vivian was a huge mistake and said as much on a number of occasions. "Viv did nothing that warranted his removal from the band in what is still considered to be a cowardly way.

---

[119] Vivian Campbell interview with James Curl.
[120] You Tube interview, Jimmy Bain.
[121] *TeamRock.com,* Dio: The Acrimonious Story Behind Holy Diver, July 10, 2016, by Mick Wall.

For me, firing Viv was the biggest mistake of Ronnie's career."

Speaking of Vivian being fired, Vinny Appice said, "Well, it was chalked down to business. There was a lot of business decisions that weren't the best for the band, and as far as the way things were cut up and stuff, so Viv had a problem with that, and Viv was more hostile toward fighting and getting what he wanted. So, he didn't see eye to with Ronnie. Eventually, that got worse and worse and worse until Ronnie said, 'I'm gonna get rid of Viv. I'm gonna get somebody else.' I didn't think it was a great decision, because Viv was part of that band, part of the magic, and a great guitar player, but it was Ronnie's band. So, yeah, it just got worse and worse and worse until one day the bubble burst and Viv's out."[122]

Claude shared his band mates' sentiment saying, "I was disappointed to see Viv undermined in the way that he was. It just seemed, to me anyway, to be manipulative and very unfair to Viv. Even though it was obvious that he was losing interest or had completely lost interest in being in the band, I still valued him as a great player and part of the identity of who the band had become. Ronnie on the other hand had grown increasingly stressed out and frustrated with Viv's isolationist behavior which in turn made for a stressful environment on the road and within the band."[123]

Being fired from Dio left the young guitarist bitterly upset and feeling betrayed. "I was very, very hurt by the way that all went down," said Vivian. "The fact that I was fired and that Ronnie reneged on his promise, and rather than uphold his end of the bargain he fired me in mid-stream literally in the middle of the tour, then

---

[122] *Blabbermouth.net*, July 4, 2012, interview with Vinny Appice, by Jeff Cramer.
[123] Claude Schnell interview with James Curl.

seamlessly brought in Craig to replace me. Not only that, but then in the immediate aftermath Ronnie goes in the press and says that I left the band, that I turned my back. He made all these excuses, like my fashion style was changing, I was listening to other sorts of music, that my heart wasn't in the band anymore."

"You know, there's some truth in that. I was wearing different clothes—why the hell not? I'm not from the generation he was from. I was listening to a lot of other music, that's true, because I was still broadening my musical horizon, I was still growing as a musician. That didn't mean that I wasn't interest in playing loud angry rock guitar. Ronnie was looking for excuses to hang the blame on me. I did not leave that band. I did not want to leave that band. I was fired. I was forced out of something I helped create, and that I put blood, sweat and tears into."[124]

Vivian also went on to say, "By the time I was fired, I was getting paid less than the lighting designer, and I was on stage playing songs that I helped write. And that's all well and good, because I was working toward that end goal, that promise."[125]

The acrimonious breakup quickly turned into a nasty war of words that lasted for years with both Ronnie and Vivian hurling verbal abuse at one another. At one point Ronnie was captured on video signing autographs and saying of Vivian, "He's a fucking asshole, he's a piece of shit." With Vivian referring to Ronnie as "one of the vilest people in the industry."

Over time, both Ronnie and Vivian softened their stance and regretted the harsh words they had spoken, with each wishing the other well. Campbell also believes that regardless of the break-up and his occasionally

---

[124] Vivian Campbell interview with James Curl.
[125] Ibid.

"awkward" relationship with Ronnie, the two would have worked together again.

"I would like to think that if Ronnie were still alive, that he and I would have been able to work together again; and I do honestly believe that. But I do also honestly believe that as long as Wendy was controlling his career, which she was until the day he died, that she would never have let that happen. But if it was just between Ronnie and I, and we never bumped into each other in 25, 28 years, but I know if we had, that at first he would have been angry because he held onto anger a lot, that was in his personality; he had a hard time letting go of anger. But once he had got done yelling at me and venting that anger we would have gone to the pub, we would have had a couple of pints and we would have gone back to his place and started jamming."[126]

For over two decades after being fired, Vivian refused to own or listen to any of the music he helped create with Ronnie; even turning off the radio if a Dio song came on. It would take years but eventually Vivian would re-embrace the incredible music he helped create.

In 2012, Campbell reconnected with Jimmy Bain, Vinny Appice and Claude Schnell and formed the band Last in Line, with singer Andrew Freeman. And although the bitter break-up still affects Vivian to this day, when asked about Ronnie he had some nice things to say, but his comments were also very truthful and telling.

"He was a nice bunch of guys, as they say," said Vivian. "Ronnie could be very engaging, he could be funny, he could be a great guy to be around. And there's other times when he could really hurt ya. One thing I will say about Ronnie, he had a real knack for discovering your Achilles heel. He really knew how to belittle people. I saw that side of him a lot, ya know, but I

---

[126] Vivian Campbell interview with James Curl.

wouldn't say that he was a bad person, not by any means."

"Like everyone, there's good and bad in all of us, and there was a lot of good in Ronnie; there was a lot of bad, too. Like I said, he did have that angry side to his personality, that vengeful side. But there were times when I did see that tender side of him. He really wanted to be like a father figure to me. And I think he took great pride in what I was doing. And he was very proud that he had brought me to the main stage, to attention through the *Holy Diver* album."

"And you know he told me many times how proud he was of me and how he thought I was a great guitar player and a great complement to his voice. You know he genuinely did care about me, but Ronnie's shell, his exterior, his guard was too ingrained in his personality, and I don't know if that was because he grew up in New York in a tough part of the world. I don't know if it's because he grew up as a short guy; you know his outside armor had to be 24/7. He never let his guard down except for those very, very few occasions, but on those few occasions when he did, he could be a very tender human being. And you know, I'm saddened that we never had a chance to make up."[127]

Out of Dio, Vivian would go on to play in Whitesnake for a short spell. From there he would eventually find a comfortable home with Def Leppard in 1993. As for Ronnie, a new era in the Dio saga was about to begin.

---

[127] Vivian Campbell interview with James Curl.

Ronnie at his grandparent's 50th wedding anniversary. Standing from left to right are Ronnie's cousins, Richard, Elain, Patty and then Ronnie, far right. Seated are Ronnie's grandmother Erminia and grandfather Anthony. Photo courtesy Bill Padavona.

Ronnie's parents Pat and Anna.
Photo courtesy of Bill Padavona.

Ronnie's mom and dad in later years.
Photo courtesy of Joey Belfiore.

Ronnie (first row, center) with his little league team. To his left is Nicky Pantas, circa 1950.
Photo courtesy of Ralph Miller.

Ronnie's boyhood home in Cortland, New York.

RONALD PADAVONA
"Pigmy"

There is no great genius without a mixture of madness.

Purple Pennant Business 3; Senior Band 1,2,3,4; Secretary 3,4; Dance Band 1,2,3,4; Orchestra 1,2; Latin Club 4; Class President 4; Noon Service Club 4; Science Club 3,4, Secretary 3, Slide-Rule Club 4; J. V. Baseball 2,3; Bowling 1; J. V. Wrestling 1,2.

Ronnie

Ronnie in high school.

Ronnie and the Red Caps. Dick Bottoff, Ronnie Padavona, Nicky Pantas and Tommy Rogers.

The Red Caps. Tommy on the drums, Dick, Ronnie and Nicky.

Ronnie, Dick, Gary and Nicky.

Ronnie, Nicky, Gary and Dick.

Ronnie, Nicky, Dick and Tommy.

Gary, Ronnie, Mickey and David.

A rare shot of Ronnie blowing the trumpet.
Photo courtesy of Bill Padavona.

The Electric Elves. Dave Feinstein, Ronnie and Gary on the drums, circa mid-60s. Photo courtesy of Bill Padavona.

Dave and Ronnie. Photo courtesy of Bill Padavona.

The Elves: Doug Thaler, Gary Driscoll, Mickey Lee Soule, Ronnie Padavona and Dave Feinstein.

The Elves: Mickey, Dave, Gary, Ronnie and Doug.

Cover of Elf's debut album, 1972. Yes, that is Ronnie as an elf. Photo by Dave Feinstein.

Gary, Ronnie, Mickey, Doug and Dave.

Ronnie, St. Alphonsus Gym, Auburn, NY, spring 1973.
Photo courtesy of Mike Donohue.

Ronnie. Photo courtesy of Mike Donohue.

Dave Feinstein, St. Alphonsus Gym, Auburn, NY, spring 1973.
Photo courtesy of Mike Donohue.

Dave. Photo courtesy of Mike Donohue.

Gary Driscoll, St. Alphonsus Gym, Auburn, NY, spring 1973. Photo courtesy of Mike Donohue.

Gary. Photo courtesy of Mike Donohue.

Mickey Lee Soule, St. Alphonsus Gym, Auburn, NY, spring 1973. Photo courtesy of Mike Donohue.

Mickey Lee, Gary Driscoll, Ronnie Padavona. St. Alphonsus Gym, Auburn, NY, spring 1973. Photo courtesy of Mike Donohue.

Ronnie, Gary, Mickey and Dave. St. Alphonsus Gym.
Photo courtesy of Mike Donohue.

Gary, Mickey, Ronnie, and Craig.

Ronnie in Courtland, New York, 1973.
Photo courtesy of Colin Hart.

Ronnie. Photo courtesy of Colin Hart.

Ronnie, Mickey and Craig Gruber.
Munich, Germany 1976. Photo courtesy of Colin Hart.

Ritchie Blackmore and Ronnie at Musicland Studio in Munich, Germany 1976. Photo courtesy of Colin Hart.

Ronnie on a flight back from London to New York, 1976. Photo courtesy of Colin Hart.

Ronnie's marriage 1978, L-R: Colin Hart, Raymond D'Addario, Ronnie, Wendy, Bob Daisley, Ritchie Blackmore, Bruce Payne and little Danny Padavona. Photo courtesy of Colin Hart.

Ronnie on stage with Gezzer and Tony, circa early 1980s.

The Hear 'n Aid crew.

Claude, Vivian, Vinny, Ronnie, Jimmy and Dean the Dragon. Sacred Heart tour 1985.
Photo by Chris Walter.

Viv, Vinny, Ronnie, Jimmy and Claude, circa 1985.

The medieval Ronnie.

Pub bar in Ronnie's house.

Ronnie's library.

Game room.

Claude Schnell.

Ronnie with a young Rowan Robertson backstage at
Hammersmith Odeon, circa 1991.
Photo courtesy of Rowan Robertson.

Ronnie and Joey Belfiore
Photo courtesy of Joey Belfiore.

Ronnie getting a trim from Joey Belfiore.
Photo courtesy of Joey Belfiore.

The domestic Ronnie.

Ronnie, hair cut by Joey Belfiore.
Photo courtesy of Joey Belfiore.

Ronnie with Niji and Sacha.

Ronnie with his beloved dogs, Niji on the left and
Buster on the right, circa mid-1980s.
Photo courtesy of Claude Schnell.

Ronnie and Colin Hart.
Photo courtesy of Colin Hart.

Ronnie and Tracy G. Sweden 1998.
Photo by Niklas Nilsson.

Doug Aldrich. Photo by Genady Perchenko.

Rudy Sarzo, Ronnie and Craig on stage in Tuska, Finland 2004. Photo by Matti Dahlbom.

Simon, Ronnie and Craig. Tuska, Finland 2004. Photo by Matti Dahlbom.

Ronnie and Craig. Photo by Matti Dahlbom.

Ronnie signing autographs at the Tuska, festival in Finland. Photo by Ari Ilvonen.

Ronnie on stage, Vinny on the drums.

Chapter Eight
Dean the Dragon

Having unceremoniously dropped Vivian from the Dio roster, Ronnie brought in Craig Goldy to take over guitar duties. Ronnie and Craig had first met back in 1982 when Craig auditioned for the guitar spot in Rough Cutt. The position had become available after Jake E. Lee defected to the Osbourne camp to replace the late Randy Rhoads. At the time of the audition, the lion-maned 21-year-old was homeless and living on the streets of L.A.

"I was living in a car," said Craig. "I was washing my hair; I had two 7UP one-liter bottles, one to rinse and I would shave with a plastic bowl and use the side-view mirror. I had a wind-up clock, because once in a while I would get a part-time job and just sleep really near it. I would use the clock to wake me up and then get dressed with my clothes in the trunk."[128]

Having grown up in a physically abusive family, Craig had been in and out of the hospital on a number of occasions. So, at 14, the young boy decided to leave home and live on the streets to avoid any more painful beatings.

Having first strummed a guitar at 13 and having grown up listening to bands like Rainbow and Sabbath, Craig's favorite singer was Ronnie. Craig found that he could relate to Ronnie's lyrics, and found solace in his voice, a voice that helped him through the difficult times in his life.

"Ronnie's was the voice that I turned to," said Craig, "because his way of writing, that kind of music kinda called to the downtrodden and black sheep of the globe, and what seemed to piss Ronnie off in his lyrics—he was very expressive when he sang, so when he sang with

---

[128] www.fullinbloommusic.com, Craig Goldy.

anger, it was about the things that angered me, too. And the things he sang where it sounded like he was sad, that was something that would make me sad too. So, I almost felt like I knew him before I even met him. And I used to learn his melody lines on guitar, and I started to notice certain things about his lyrics."[129]

On the night Craig auditioned for Rough Cutt, Ronnie and Wendy had to rent gear for the young musician; without a home and nearly penniless all he had was a guitar.

"They had to find me, too," said Craig. "How do you find a kid that lives in his car? But I had made a demo, with the last $20 I made from giving guitar lessons, and a friend of mine moved to L.A. and the band he joined was friends with Rough Cutt, so my demo got into Ronnie's hands. And there were all these guitar players who were ready to go, with all their stage clothes and equipment, reputations already built, but there was something in that demo that made Ronnie say, 'We gotta get this kid up here.' So, I get the phone call the night before, saying that Ronnie wants to meet at the audition, he wants to meet you. He wants to meet *me*? I'm the one who wants to meet *him*! But there he was, the man. I still get chills thinking about it. And we started talking before the audition, and he told me, 'Don't be so overwhelmed. I'm a fan of what you do, too. I really loved the songs and the way you played on that demo. That's why you're here tonight.'"

"So, I told him that his lyrics, when I was learning his melody lines on the guitar, he often seemed like he would say one thing and mean another, like polarizing evil and good at once, and he grabbed my arm and said, 'Yes! Yes!' almost like I'd cracked his code or something. And little did I know that night, right there,

---

[129] *burningambulance.com, July 19, 2017 interview*Craig *Goldy.*

was the beginning of a 30-plus year friendship and working relationship, because I understood him so well. Even when he was in Heaven & Hell, he would call me at home and say, 'Goldy, Goldy, you gotta hear this,' and he would read me his lyrics, 'cause he knew I knew what they would mean. So, he was the producer of Rough Cutt, and we would work in the studio together, and often it would be just him and me and the engineer, finishing things up, and one night he looked at me and said, 'Goldy, if Vivian Campbell ever doesn't work out, you'll be my first choice.' And that's why there were no auditions when Vivian was out and I was in, because he was a man of his word. We had been friends, and we'd worked together in the studio so many times together that we knew it would work."[130]

With Craig as the new guitarist, the band headed over to Europe to resume the *Sacred Heart* tour. After a month abroad, they were back in the States in May where they continued on with the third leg of the tour.

At this point in time Dio was at the absolute peak of their popularity and the band was selling out huge shows in both Europe and the U.S. Over the years, as Dio's fame and success had grown, so had their stage show. The theatrics had become bigger and increasingly extravagant, as well as visually stunning. Speaking of the shows, Ronnie remarked, "I like things that move, I like things that come alive, I like dragons that come alive, pyramids that tops come off, robots that move, three-headed snakes that fight each other. That to me that is what Disneyland is all about and that's what I always try to bring to the people at the shows. We brought 'Dio Land' to them."[131]

---

[130] *burningambulance.com, July 19, 2017 interview*Craig *Goldy.*
[131] You Tube Interview by Michael Eriksson 2001.

Claude, who was there during all the glory, remembers the magnificence of the shows, saying, "There was a dragon and knights that would battle. It was like a heavy metal Disneyland."

Being that the show was so popular, it made sense to use it for as long as possible. Despite the big stage production and added expense of hauling such a massive stage set from state to state, Ronnie didn't raise the ticket prices. This cut into his profits somewhat, but as long as the fans were happy, that's all that mattered to him.

One particular stop on the tour that Ronnie enjoyed was the Spectrum arena in Philadelphia on June 17, 1986. For a huge sports fan like Ronnie it was exciting to play in such a renowned sports mecca. The Spectrum show was also filmed and not only captured Dio at the peak of their powers, but the massive *Sacred Heart* stage production as well. The concert was later released as a live DVD.

The Spectrum show began with an opening keyboard intro while the crowd waited anxiously with thousands of cigarette lighters waving. The rock wall under Vinny's drums, which sat atop a ten-foot riser, slowly opened. A moment later, amidst laser lights, smoke and explosions of multi-colored sparks, Ronnie rushed onto the stage. On cue, the band launched full throttle into "The King of Rock 'n' Roll," and the crowed went crazy.

About halfway through the set list the theatrical part of the stage show began. A large round screen lowered from above and came to rest on the stage. A holographic image of Ronnie's face was displayed and in a resounding voice he said to the enthralled audience, "Greetings my children. Come with me now and discover the magic that lives below the sea of dreams… and if you have courage to cross the rainbow bridge, you many find the Sacred Heart." Ronnie's face then disappeared in a wreath of bright orange flames and an instant later the band jumped into the song "Sacred Heart."

The centerpiece of this part of the show was a 20-foot mechanical dragon affectionately known as Dean. The massive animatronic beast loomed over the medieval, castle-like stage set with blazing red eyes and razor-tipped fangs. During the song Ronnie would take his laser light sword and engage in mock battle with the giant beast. All the while Dean would roar loudly while breathing fiery sparks and shooting red lasers from his eyes. Ronnie would eventually slay the dragon, with its chest splitting open to reveal the mystical "Sacred Heart." To say the least the exhibition was visually pleasing, and the crowd responded with deafening approval.

As one might imagine, having a huge dragon and such an extensive stage set required a lot of hard work. To put Dean and the stage props up each night took a crew of about 50 people. Moreover, having a mechanical dragon provided more than one anecdote that would have fit right into the *Spinal Tap* movie. For example, when Dean would breathe a shower of sizzling sparks some of them would land on the stage floor where they would often continue to smolder and burn. Whichever band member was nearest at the time would make their way over and step on it before the stage caught fire.

During the show everyone got a moment to shine with a solo. Vinny, towering over the stage on his riser, pounded the skins with drum sticks that were lit up with red LED lights. His thunderous hammering and energetic performance got the crowd fired up.

Craig was also given ample time to display his skills on the six-string and did a fine job. During his solo the virtuoso showed a mastery over his instrument with a plethora of tricks and blinding speed that left the crowd awe-struck.

Even the keyboard player got a moment to shine, something that wasn't typical in a metal band. Claude, like Vinny, also sat atop a riser, shaped like a stone castle tower. Although he had played the majority of the first two Dio tours offstage, his keyboard obbligatos were always an integral part of the shows. And though it had taken some time for Claude to come out from behind the curtains, by the *Sacred Heart* tour he was on stage full-time. With the spotlight shining, his essential musical textures and melodies were augmented by an extended keyboard solo that had the audience rockin' and was by all accounts a spectacle to behold.

The enormously successful *Sacred Heart* tour wrapped up in October of 1986. A few months later work began on the *Dream Evil* album, Dio's fourth record and the first without Campbell. Recording for the album went well, however by this time Ronnie had tightened his grip on the band as well as his control over the musical direction and creative input. While this didn't bother Craig, who hadn't been in the band long, Vinny resented the lack of creativity.

"In the beginning anything went," said Vinny, "and that's the way it should be. Like 'I got this crazy idea, let's do this' and we tried it, and he [Ronnie] would go with it and start singing and write stuff. The word 'can't' wasn't in there. Then as each album went along it got not so much fun."[132]

While Vinny found Ronnie's control smothering, Claude was given a rare opportunity and free reign to create a keyboard solo for the song "All the Fools Sailed Away." This was something that had never been done before on a Dio album and was a big deal for Claude. As

---

[132] You Tube interview, Vinny Appice.

the band had evolved, Claude's keyboards had become more prevalent and Ronnie felt that the time was right.

Feeling as if he carried the weight of all keyboardists trying to get noticed, Claude labored for weeks perfecting and tweaking his solo until he was ready to record. Showing up at the studio Claude found that Ronnie and Angelo were already there and everything was set up and ready to go. Jumping right onto the keyboards Claude warmed up by playing the solo in its entirety.

"So, I'm going through it and I finish it and Ronnie looks at Angelo and says, 'Did you get that?'"

"'Yeah,' replies Angelo."

"Ronnie turns to me and gives me the thumbs up and says with a smile, 'I love it! Can you do it again?' I'm like sure, is that the one we're going to keep? 'Why not?' asks Ronnie. 'I don't know, you're the producer,' and he goes, 'Well let's listen to it.' So, we listened to it and maybe it was because I wasn't expecting Angelo to record, or I was just thinking it was a practice run so I wasn't paying attention to how well or not well I did and it was fine and Ronnie goes, 'What did you think?' 'Yeah, if you're okay, I'm okay,' and he replied, 'It's fucking spectacular.' So, the very first take I did was the take that ended up on the record."[133]

Ronnie's enthusiastic response to Claude's playing stands as one of his most memorable moments, both personally and professionally.

With the keyboard solo done, the rest of the guys got to hear it. Everyone was impressed, particularly Craig, who felt that a reworking of his guitar solo was necessary so he wouldn't be overshadowed.

Heavy metal and Dio were still riding high when *Dream Evil* hit the record racks in mid-1987. Despite the

---

[133] Claude Schnell interview with James Curl.

blow of losing a core member in Vivian, the album turned out surprisingly well. The cover art also featured the return of Murray, Dio's demon-like mascot.

"I thought it was a good album," said Claude, "certainly better than *Sacred Heart*. I was very happy with that record; I thought Craig did a really great job. I have great memories of the *Dream Evil* album. It was a fun record to make."

Fan response was mostly positive and from the LP came two big singles, "I Could Have Been a Dreamer" and the epic ballad, "All the Fools Sailed Away." Although there are noticeably more keyboards on the album, they're not used to give the songs a more "radio-friendly" sound. Instead, Claude's masterful playing helps accent, and in some cases create a more ominous atmosphere on tracks like "Dream Evil," "Naked in the Rain" and "All the Fools Sailed Away." Overall the album is well done and Ronnie seemed to have a creative spurt when he teamed up with Craig.

Along with the album came videos for the singles, "All the Fools Sailed Away" and "I Could Have Been a Dreamer." Claude, who remembers filming the videos, recalls a funny incident that happened while shooting "I Could Have Been a Dreamer."

"The big thing about shooting that video," said Claude, "was that we were going to have live wolves running through the set. There was an animal control truck parked out back and Sheila (Claude's wife) and I put our faces up to the louvers to see inside the cage. And when those things came running to the back, oh man! I'm lucky I wasn't standing in a puddle of pee, they were so aggressive and feral."[134]

Continuing, Claude said, "The parameters for using live animals in any kind of production are exceedingly

---

[134] Claude Schnell interview with James Curl.

strict. They're scheduled for a certain time, they arrive at a certain time and they're fed in accordance to whatever time they say you're going to need them. And if you don't need them on time or you're running late, and they haven't been fed, well, they get fed. The health and welfare of the animal comes first, as is typical with any type of Hollywood production. To Wendy's default she should have known that and scheduled accordingly. But the time for the wolf shoot came and went and the wolves hadn't been fed and they wanted to shoot the scene before they were fed, because apparently once they eat they become lethargic, which they did. Once they got fed they basically just kinda laid down and looked around. The trainer handling the wolves could barely get them to do anything."

"So, what you see in the video is a severely-edited, multiple takes of the wolves barely walking through the set. They also did some film acceleration to make them look like they were running. But I'll tell you what, the animals they were before they ate had no reflection on the animals they were after they ate."[135]

In August of 1987, Dio began their *Dream Evil* tour by playing a benefit concert for the Children of the Night charity foundation. The show was held at the Irvine Meadows theatre and was recorded and later released as a two-CD set, with all the profits going to the charity.

From there Ronnie and the boys headed over to Europe for five months. Although the stage show for the *Dream Evil* tour didn't have a dragon or knights it was still fantasy-based. There were giant bats that would fly around and at one point a huge mechanical spider would come down from above with its long, slender legs flailing. Craig, while playing his guitar solo, would shoot

---

[135] Claude Schnell interview with James Curl

the spider with a laser from his guitar, killing the giant arachnid.

By December, Dio was back in America playing with Megadeth and Savatage. They finished up the *Dream Evil* tour three months later in March of 1988. Following the eight months of continuous touring, everyone took a well-deserved rest.

A few months after the *Dream Evil* tour ended, Ronnie made a decision to fire Jimmy Bain. It was a difficult decision and one that he had been wrestling with for some time; he and Jimmy had been friends and band mates for over a decade. Jimmy's personal problems, coupled with the fact that it was costing Ronnie a lot of money to help keep him in the country had finally reached a breaking point. For support, Ronnie had Claude come over to accompany him.

Claude arrived at Ronnie's house and spent some time playing with Buster, Ronnie's Doberman pinscher. They were just getting ready to leave when the phone suddenly rang. Ronnie answered and said, "This is Ronnie. Oh, hi Craig." For a few moments the two talked. "All I heard," said Claude, "was Ronnie saying, 'Really, I see. And you're quite sure about this? No, no you don't need to say anything else, that's fine, okay bye.'" Hanging up the phone, Ronnie turned to Claude and said with some surprise, "Craig just quit the band." Both guys were shocked and later learned that Craig went to join up with the band Driver.

With Craig having made an unexpected exit, Ronnie put off firing Jimmy. He knew from experience that finding a guitarist would be hard enough without having to find a bass player as well. With the sudden turn of events, Ronnie focused his attention on finding a replacement for Craig.

Chapter Nine
Lock up the Wolves
And Sabbath Once More

With Craig out of the band, Ronnie began the hunt for a new guitar player. Over in Cambridge, England 17-year old guitar phenom Rowan Robertson had heard the rumors that Dio was looking. Ambitiously, the young boy sent a tape to Dio's record label, Phonogram Records, and waited. A few months later he got a response saying that they weren't interested in him at the moment. Encouraged by his best friend Sean Manning, who would eventually play guitar for the band Hurricane, Rowan didn't give up. He contacted the Dio fan club and was told to send in a demo tape, which he promptly did.

Back in America, Ronnie and Vinny had been spending weeks listening to thousands of demo tapes, while auditioning various guitar players. Claude, who remembered some of the auditions said, "Most of the guitar players were just awful. They would come in with the standard 1980s rocker look—spandex and big hair like Nikki Sixx from Mötley Crüe and you could tell they hadn't done their homework. A lot of them didn't know the songs all the way through."[136]

On one particular occasion, a relatively unknown guitarist named Gary Hoey tried out for the band. Unlike most of the other axemen, Gary showed up wearing jeans, a t-shirt, flip-flops and had short blond hair. "I had heard there was an audition," said Gary. "It was Claude who got me in. I had sent Ronnie a cassette tape with a couple of demos on it and he liked my writing, he liked

---

[136] Claude Schnell interview with James Curl.

my riffs and he liked some of the ideas I had musically. And I remember Ronnie wanted me to teach the band the song I had written. I remember coming in to rehearsal and showing the guys how it went and it was really cool. He let me try out one of my songs with the band and we goofed around for a while."

"I remember he was really cool, super nice and really gracious. I remember we played 'Last in Line;' that was one that really stood out to me, great song. And if you get to play it with Ronnie, I mean whether I got the gig or not it was an incredible experience to play with him and Jimmy Bain and everybody. I will say this. When Ronnie came in to do the audition he could sing. It was just like an album—it was like WOW! Not holding back, not hitting bad notes. I was just blown away how he just walked in and sang his ass off. I just think he was truly one of the greatest rock singers of all time."[137]

Claude, who remembers the audition well, said, "Gary was by far the best guitarist we auditioned. He blew the fucking roof off the place! He knew the songs, he had done his homework. We jammed for about two hours and Vinny was covered in sweat and smiling. After the audition we all felt that Gary was the answer to our need for a guitar player." Ronnie however, had different plans. He had already discovered Rowan Robertson, the guitarist that he wanted and had no intention of hiring Gary.

Following the jam session, Ronnie walked Gary to his car and when he came back he said, "I know this isn't what you guys want to hear, but he's not the guy for us." Understandably, Vinny, Claude and Jimmy were extremely disappointed.

When asked years later why he thought he didn't get the gig, Gary said, "I think, in a way Ronnie found the

---

[137] Gary Hoey interview with James Curl.

new young prodigy (Rowan Robertson). I think he was sort of taking a tip from Ozzy Osbourne, in discovering the new younger guy."[138]

Years later, when Gary had a top five hit with the song "Hocus Pocus" from the *Animal Instinct* album, he ran into Ronnie. "I remember Ronnie saying to me, 'Gary, I'm really happy for you; you deserve all your success.'"[139]

It was while going through a mountain of about 5,000 cassette tapes that Ronnie had come across Rowan's demo. Having such an experienced ear, Ronnie knew instantly that Rowan was something special, so he had Wendy call the young guitarist.

It had been several months since Rowan had sent his demo to the Dio fan club, so he was a little surprised and shocked when he got a call from Wendy one night at about eight o'clock. The two talked for a while and she asked him if he would like to play in front of 20,000 people. Being a bit of a cocky kid, Rowan replied nonchalantly, "Well, alright, I guess."

Wendy told him that Ronnie would really like to see him play. She then asked if he would like to come out to Los Angeles and audition. Excited and a little nervous, Rowan agreed to make the trip. Excitedly the boy told his parents the incredible news. Rowan's dad, happy for his son's good fortune, gave his boy some words of wisdom saying, "Look, you're getting a free vacation to play with your heroes in Los Angeles, so it's already a good situation, so just have fun."[140]

In February of 1989 the 17-year-old guitarist was flown to Los Angeles where he auditioned. It was an unusual situation the teenager found himself in,

---

[138] Ibid.
[139] Ibid.
[140] The Metal Voice, you tube interview with Rowan Robertson, July 16, 2015.

surrounded by band mates who were old enough to be his father. Around the rehearsal studio everyone had heard about the young virtuoso and wanted a peek. Even David Coverdale, who had heard the rumors about the young hotshot, couldn't resist stopping by Ronnie's studio. Upon seeing the baby-faced six-stringer, Coverdale asked, "How old is this guy, 12?" After David had left, Rowan jokingly remarked to Ronnie that he should have told Coverdale, "I'm the age you wish you were."[141]

As usual, Ronnie did his best to make the new guy comfortable and wasted no time setting Rowan up with a nickname. "My first nickname given to me by Ronnie was 'Shnick.' This happened because at my audition over there in The Alley rehearsal rooms on Lankershim Boulevard, I was setting up my pedals and guitar, ready to play the first notes with the man. Ronnie said to me—I remember it well—'I really want this to work.' Always gave me his confidence and bolstered up my self-belief."

"Anyway, there I was setting up my pedals and fiddling with things ready to go, when I managed to trip myself up on my own gear and nearly fall off the stage. Ronnie looked over from his place of preparation behind the center stage mic and calls, 'Oh great, we've got Baryshnikov over here.' Baryshnikov of course being a famous ballet dancer. From then on my name was Shnick."[142]

The first audition went well for Rowan. "I remember looking over and seeing Jimmy Bain smiling away, and I thought, 'I must be doing something right.'"[143]

---

[141] Rowan Robertson interview with James Curl.
[142] Themetealden.com, Rowan Robertson remembers Dio, May 26, 2010.
[143] YouTube interview, Rowan Robertson.

Following the rehearsal, Ronnie knew he had found his guitarist. A few days later Rowan was brought back to audition again and invited to join the band.

As an official member of Dio, arrangements were made for the boy to stay in the Los Angeles. Larry Morand, who was Ronnie's assistant, agreed to let Rowan move into his apartment and the two became fast friends. Larry took Rowan to parties and on hiking trips. Ronnie jokingly called it "Camp Larr" and told Larry that Rowan had better not break a wrist while hiking.

After Rowan was made an official member of Dio, Ronnie and Wendy sat down with the young guitarist and laid out some ground rules. One of the rules was no drugs, particularly cocaine. Recalling the conversation, Rowan said, "They told me, 'If you go anywhere near cocaine we will kill you.'"[144] This didn't however stop Rowan from drinking. In no time the boy was introduced to the Rainbow club where Jimmy Bain gave the young guitarist his second nickname, "Mr. Vomit."

Back in England, Rowan's parents were happy to hear that their son had gotten the gig, but were nevertheless a little worried about their 17-year-old boy being in the big city of Los Angeles. Rowan's dad John came out to visit and he and Ronnie had a sit-down. Ronnie assured Rowan's father that he was watching out for his boy and he was well taken care of.

Once Rowan was settled in, work began on a new album titled *Lock up the Wolves*. At first Rowan was a little apprehensive about writing, but Ronnie reassured him that he would do great. He then explained that he wanted Rowan to come up with guitar riffs that they could build songs from.

"Ronnie used to like to work from a riff first which usually he came to his guitar player for," said Rowan.

---

[144] Rowan Robertson interview with James Curl, January 28, 2017.

"So, what I would have to do was come up with loads of riffs and play them one by one. Then what we would do is play, jam the riff and sit there and stand and go, 'Where can we take it; anyone got any ideas?' We would record them on a boom box and Ronnie would take them home overnight and come up with let's say a vocal melody or he might already have titles sitting around. I remember he came in once and he said, 'I've got a title for the album, *Lock up the Wolves.*' Ronnie wrote with the band all the time; he used to say this type of music comes from a band in a room."[145]

Rowan did his best but could tell at times Ronnie would get frustrated with him. Looking back now, he could see that it was no doubt because he was so young.

"I was already a good guitarist," said Rowan, "but I wish I could have worked with Ronnie when I was a little older, because I got a lot better."[146]

It was about halfway through the ten-month writing process of the album that everything came crashing down, causing a major lineup change. "There was a lot of unhappiness in the band during this time," said Claude. "Vinny was talking about leaving and I felt that without Vinny, there was really no reason for me to stay."[147] Furthermore, the guys were still resentful that Ronnie had passed on Gary. And although Rowan was a brilliant guitarist, they were having a hard time relating to and working with the teenage boy. "We were seasoned adults," said Claude, "and Rowan was literally wet behind the ears."[148]

The catalyst that sparked the lineup change took place during a rehearsal session. Ronnie got frustrated at Rowan for missing some notes. "To be fair," said Claude, "Ronnie was a severe task-master, and it wasn't

---

[145] Brave worlds interview with Rowan Robertson, July 16, 2015.
[146] Ibid.
[147] Claude Schnell interview with James Curl.
[148] Ibid

surprising that Rowan had a hard time keeping the songs in the right order and remembering which parts Ronnie wanted changed." Pissed off, the fiery singer blew up and started cussing. Vinny, Claude and Rowan rested quietly behind their respective instruments—Vinny fiddling with his drumsticks.

As Ronnie shouted angrily at Rowan, Jimmy decided to make light of the situation. He stood behind Ronnie out of sight and began mocking and making fun of him. Unable to control himself, Claude started laughing at Jimmy's antics. Noticing that Claude was laughing, Ronnie shouted, "What the fuck are you laughing at?!" He then wheeled around quickly sensing that something was up. Jimmy, who was stoned at the time, was too slow to react and was caught.

"There was no acting his way out," said Claude. Realizing that Jimmy was making fun of him, Ronnie got even angrier. "Ronnie was seething with anger," said Claude. Furious, Ronnie grabbed his things and stormed out of the studio while shouting a few choice swear words at his band mates. "Well," said Vinny, "I guess that's the end of rehearsal for today."[149]

The next day Claude got a call from Wendy saying that rehearsals were canceled until further notice and that she wanted to see him at her office. Once there, Wendy informed Claude that she had heard what happened at rehearsal. As a result, Jimmy Bain had been fired and bassist Teddy Cook was being brought in as his replacement.

She then explained that Ronnie was very upset and expected Claude to make a full apology or he would be fired as well. Feeling he did nothing wrong, Claude said he would not apologize. He then made it clear that if anyone was going to apologize it would be Ronnie. Wendy then told Claude that his services were no longer

---

[149] Claude Schnell interview with James Curl.

needed and that they would be bringing in Jens Johansson to replace him.

With Jimmy and Claude officially out of the band, Vinny hung in for a few weeks longer but eventually decided to leave. He was replaced by former AC/DC drummer Simon Wright, and it was truly the end of an era. A few weeks later Ronnie called Claude and apologized and the two parted as friends.

With a new band quickly assembled, work continued on *Lock up the Wolves*. Once the album was written, Dio headed over to Reno for six weeks of recording at Granny's House recording studio. From there Ronnie and his band mates headed over to England to mix the album and ready themselves for a world tour.

Lock up the Wolves was released on May 15, 1990, and was loaded with some very good tracks, like "Hey Angel," "Wild One" and "Why Are They Watching Me?" Sound-wise the album is a departure from Dio's previous efforts and lyrically it steers away from medieval-themed songs. The record is heavily guitar-driven and Rowan's playing is refreshing and sensational, while Ronnie's voice, even at 48, is as powerful as ever.

Fan reaction, however, was split. Some found it "energetic, entertaining and diverse" while older fans who grew up with *Holy Diver* and *Last in Line* were put off by the album's noticeably thicker, slower sound. But, overall, reviews were generally positive.

While *Lock up the Wolves* was certainly a solid album, it was overshadowed somewhat by a new kind of music that was starting to engulf the youth of America. The music scene and industry were undergoing some drastic changes and the popularity of hard rock and heavy metal was starting to wane. A new generation was coming of age along with a new kind of music called grunge that was about to hit like a musical tidal wave. Like he had years before in the 1960s, Ronnie was about to witness another big change in musical direction; grunge was about to hit big and kick everyone's ass.

Grunge or the "Seattle Sound," as it is sometimes referred to, originated in Seattle, Washington during the mid-1980s and came from a mixture of punk, post-punk and '70s hard rock. The first bands to gain wide-spread international attention were Nirvana and Pearl Jam with their 1991 releases of *Nevermind* and *Ten* respectively. Alice in Chains broke huge with their second album, 1992's *Dirt* and suddenly grunge became the most popular form of heavy music across the globe.

Other grunge bands like Soundgarden and Stone Temple Pilots were also commercially successful. In no time grunge's popularity, along with rap, eclipsed hair metal and traditional forms of heavy metal.

Dio embarked on a relatively short tour of only five months in support of *Lock up the Wolves*. The band's first show was as the opener for Metallica and took place on May 16, 1990 in the city of Zwolle, Netherlands. Rowan, who had only played in front of about a hundred people before joining Dio, did well. When asked if he was nervous playing his first show in front of 7,000 screaming fans, he said, "No," then added, "I think, I didn't know how shocked I was. I was a kid thinking, 'This is life? Cool.'"[150]

The relatively short length of the tour, only five months, no doubt had something to do with the fact that Ronnie had plans to rejoin Black Sabbath. It was while on the tour that Geezer had joined Dio on stage to play "Neon Knights" at Roy Wilkins Auditorium in Minneapolis, Minnesota. And that's all it took.

Following the show, Ronnie and Geezer hung out and inevitably their conversation turned to talks about Ronnie getting back together with Sabbath; essentially making a reunion out of it. A couple days later Geezer spoke with Tony and expressed how great it felt to play

---

[150]Rowan Robertson interview with James Curl.

with Ronnie, and from there the wheels were set in motion. For the past few years Sabbath had been in a musical lull. They had gone through several lineup changes and their last couple of albums had been less than outstanding. The decision to reunite with Ronnie was an easy one.

Once Ronnie's decision to rejoin Sabbath was final, Dio was disbanded. Rowan recalls the time, saying, "I was a little surprised, I guess. But I wasn't at all upset about it. I was told by Wendy that Ronnie was putting the band on ice and that he was going to work with Sabbath again and that she would pursue other avenues for me. It ended up that I wanted to do my own project so she hooked me up with Oni Logan and our band was called Violet's Demise."[151]

With Dio on hold, Ronnie and Tony got together and formulated plans for a new album. Tony knew that having Ronnie back in the band was a good move because the two worked and created together very well. There was only one problem. Ronnie had drummer Simon Wright that he wanted to use and Tony had Cozy Powell. Eventually, Cozy was chosen to play, but Ronnie wasn't happy since he and Cozy were never the best of friends. Even when they played together years before in Rainbow their relationship was tense.

The animosity between Ronnie and Cozy made early work on the album difficult. At one point Cozy warned Tony saying, "If that little cunt says anything to me, I'm going to smash him in the face!"[152] As a result of the tension, Ronnie abruptly quit at one point and flew back to Los Angeles. Singer Tony Martin was brought in and began rehearsing with the band. However, after cooling

---

[151] Ibid.
[152] Ironman, My Journey through Heaven and Hell with Black Sabbath, by Tony Iommi with T.J. Lammers, Da Capo Press, 2011.

off, Ronnie returned a few weeks later. And then, as fate would have it, Cozy was injured when a horse he was riding had a heart attack and suddenly died. As the animal fell it landed on Cozy, breaking the drummer's hip and putting him on the couch and away from his drums for months. To take the unlucky drummer's place, Vinny Appice was brought in.

"If it wasn't such a horrible thing to say," said Tony, "you could call the accident a blessing in disguise. I love Cozy and he was a great friend, but you have to have the right combination in the band. We already had enough friction going on with everything anyway, so we needed to have something stable. Getting Vinny back was the obvious answer to all our problems."[153]

Although Ronnie was feeling upbeat with Vinny back in the band, work on what would become the *Dehumanizer* album continued to be difficult and tedious and the boys didn't always get along. At times, when Ronnie was feeling frustrated with Sabbath, he would jokingly refer to the band as "Back Stabbath."

As work on the album progressed there was a tremendous amount of pressure on the band to put out an exceptional piece of work. As a result, the guys spent a lot of time changing and analyzing each song from every conceivable angle. To add more stress, Tony had asked Ronnie to refrain from singing about "dungeons and dragons and rainbows."

Caught off guard by the request, Ronnie was a little put off saying, "I've always used rainbows."[154] To which Tony replied, "Well, you know, we think it's a bit much."[155] After some tense moments, Ronnie relented and agreed to rethink his lyrical practices.

---

[153] Ibid.
[154] Ibid.
[155] Ibid.

Finally, after months of hard work the band went into the recording studio at Rockfield Studios in Wales. Recording took about six weeks and by all accounts went smoothly. A few weeks later the album was released on June 22, 1992, and it did not disappoint. It did however, suffer a bit from the same fate as *Lock up the Wolves*, namely that it was somewhat overlooked because of the massive popularity of grunge.

With all the new and exciting music from younger bands coming out such as Alice in Chains, Stone Temple Pilots, Pantera and Rage Against the Machine, it's easy to see how a next generation of hard rock fans overlooked it. Still, the album was well received by fans who were inclined to be curious about Black Sabbath.

Lyrically and musically, *Dehumanizer* is a true doom metal album and arguably the heaviest record Sabbath ever put out. Getting away from the medieval metaphors, Ronnie's lyrics cover a wide range of more contemporary subjects, for example, dealing with the misuse of technology.

As a unit, the reformed band—this was the exact lineup that had constructed 1981's *Mob Rules* record—proved to be exceptionally tight. Tony's heavy riffs are powerful while Geezer and Vinny are both in top-form. Although the album did well, managing to peak at #44 on the Billboard 200 chart, it wasn't a massive hit. Instead, it has become one of those rare gems that many missed at the time, but are happy when they discover it.

"We wanted it to be real rock 'n' roll, real basic," said Ronnie. "We wanted to capture what we are live and that's really what I think we did. We didn't do tons of overdubs or a lot of chorus-y kind of things. I think the important thing is that a band should be able to do all the things they do on record live, without any kind of sampling crap or that rubbish—so, of course, we didn't.

We recorded it true to what the band is: just guitar, bass, drums and vocals, y'know—a couple of keyboard things here and there."[156]

To commemorate the album, Sabbath took off on a tour starting in June of 1992 in Sao Paulo, Brazil. The campaign concluded five months later in November at the Kaiser Convention Center in Oakland, California—and then everything fell apart.

In late 1992, Ozzy Osbourne announced that he would be retiring from performing. His farewell gigs were going to be played on the 14th and 15th of November at the Pacific Amphitheater in Costa Mesa, California. Tony was asked if Sabbath would perform at the shows, to which he readily agreed, because he genuinely believed that Ozzy was retiring for good. The deal was Sabbath would open for Ozzy and then switch and do three songs at the end of Ozzy's show with the original lineup of Black Sabbath. "We thought it would be a nice gesture to do it,"[157] said Tony.

Ronnie however, had very different feelings about opening for Ozzy. In the past there had been a lot of negative talk between the two camps, with both sides having said some very nasty things. Because of this, Ronnie, ever the consummate "band guy," felt that he and his band had been insulted. So, in his typical direct manner, the incorrigible singer gave his answer saying, "No! I will not open for someone who has treated us that badly. I'm not supporting a clown."[158]

Ronnie's answer was unyielding, and final. Unwilling to take the stage, Rob Halford was brought in. And as quickly as that, Ronnie and Vinny once again found themselves fellow outcasts from Black Sabbath.

---

[156] WERS-*Nasty Habits*, recorded at New York's China Club.
[157] Ibid.
[158] Ibid.

Chapter Ten
Dio Once Again

"I had a talk with Ronnie about his voice one time, and he said he felt like he had the Grand Canyon at the back of his throat." Jeff Pilson

After the short-lived Black Sabbath reunion, Ronnie and Vinny decided to re-form Dio. A quick call was made to Jimmy Bain and they had a bass player.

The trio then turned their attention to getting a new axeman. At first, their plan was to have an all-star band of sorts, so Ronnie called several big-name guitar players like Neal Schon, Vinny Moore, Michael Schenker and Yngwie Malmsteen, all of whom were tied up with projects or tours.

Vinny then suggested Tracy Grijalva, a.k.a. Tracy G., a guitarist he and Jimmy had played with in the band World War III in 1991. Vinny played Ronnie some of Tracy's music, but Ronnie was initially reluctant. Tracy used a lot of sound effects and was a vastly different guitarist than Ritchie, Tony, Craig, Rowan or Vivian. Nevertheless, Ronnie trusted his band mates and agreed to have Tracy come in for an audition.

A few days later the boys met at a rehearsal studio where Tracy, Jimmy and Vinny played some songs for Ronnie. Although Tracy had been part of the music scene in L.A. for years and had played with Vinny and Jimmy, it was the first time he had ever met Ronnie. Having been a big fan since he was a kid, Tracy was understandably a little awed by the singer, but despite this, the audition went well. And since the three had played together previously they were familiar with each other's style and the music came easily.

"The one thing Ronnie noticed right away," said Tracy, "was it instantly sounded like Dio's band got a lot fucking heavier." Although the initial audition went well, Ronnie wasn't sold on Tracy, so he scheduled another. "A month went by," said Tracy, "then Vinny called me again and said, 'Ronnie wants you to come back and play some more.'" After the second audition Ronnie told Tracy that he would call him in a few days. Two days later Tracy got a call from Vinny who said excitedly, "Tell your dad you're the new guitar player for Dio." Tracy's reaction was, "Wow! I didn't think I would get the gig. Things like that don't happen to guys like me. It was like hitting the musical lottery."[159]

After hiring Tracy, Ronnie then brought keyboardist Scott Warren aboard. Scott would remain a consistent member of the band for the next 17-seventeen-years, making him the second longest-standing member behind Ronnie himself.

After being made an official member of Dio, Ronnie offered Tracy a room in his spacious house so the two could be close and work together undisturbed. Arriving at Ronnie's place, he gave Tracy the choice of four different rooms saying, "Pick a room."

After moving in, Tracy was impressed with the extraordinary house and asked Ronnie if he could bring his parents over for a tour. "Sure," replied Ronnie, "bring 'em down here." A few days later Tracy had his parents over. Ronnie, having been raised in a Catholic Italian home had been taught to revere family elders and it was no different with Tracy's parents. "He was very respectful and treated them like a king and queen," said Tracy. Ronnie then proceeded to give them the grand

---

[159] Interview with Tracy Grijalva with James Curl, December 22, 2016.

tour of his home which was affectionately known as "the castle house."

Ronnie had bought the house shortly after the release of the *Sacred Heart* album in September of '85 and moved in with his German shepherd Niji. By the mid-'80s Ronnie had several successful tours behind him and platinum albums adorning his walls. As a result of his hard work and success he had become a very wealthy man. With his musical earnings he purchased the five-bedroom, five-bath mansion that was just over 5,000 square feet. At the time it had cost a little more than $750,000. Today it would sell for about $3,000,000.

The house was built in 1981 in the style of an English manor and rested on a large lot in the affluent neighborhood of Encino, California. Inside, the home's furnishings reflected Ronnie's personality and meticulous nature. It was decorated with exotic antiques and fine hand-crafted furniture that expressed Ronnie's love of the medieval.

There were walls adorned with swords, armor and finely wrought candelabrums as well as expensive paintings. The antiquated décor and Old World charm gave one the feeling that they had stepped back to a more chivalrous time. One particular piece, an old wooden chest, was made in 1495 and once resided in the royal residence of Windsor castle, in England.

Other custom original pieces included 200-year-old hardwood floors from France and a pub bar built in 1820 from the Kings Arms in Chiqwell, England. The house also featured custom stained antique windows from the 18th & 19th centuries, as well as vintage cathedral windows, crafted in 1790, in the master bedroom.

To entertain guests, Ronnie also had a game room with an elaborate hand-carved pool table that was a Christmas gift from Wendy. The room also featured a massive fireplace to keep everyone warm, hand-made tapestries and beautiful marble floors. Tracy's parents were especially impressed with the large walk-in closets and how spotless his house was.

"As for Ronnie's house," said Jeff Pilson, "it was beyond immaculate and he was the housekeeper! He could never trust getting a cleaning person as he had so many valuable knick-knacks all over his house, and they were in very specific places, so he only trusted himself to keep it neat and tidy. And believe me it was always neat and tidy!"[160]

A great lover of books, Ronnie also had an extensive library with high wall-mounted shelves filled with hundreds of volumes. As an insatiable reader, Ronnie would often partake of his library where he could be found relaxing with a good book and a pint of dark beer. One particular piece of interest on display was a very old Bible resting on a Bible box.

Across from the library was the dining room. It boasted a large, lavishly made table with baroquely carved high-back chairs, a stunning crystal chandelier and beautiful hand-painted griffin wallpaper. And, as one would expect, the home also came with a heated pool and a fully-functional studio called "the dungeon." It was here that Ronnie and his band mates would often come up with ideas and record. "I wrote the riff to 'Hunter of the Heart' and demoed it there," said Tracy.

It was shortly after Tracy moved in that the band had its first meeting, with everyone eating dinner at the big dining table. Wendy, along with Jeff, Vinny and Jimmy, was there explaining that the band would be booking shows in South America, Japan and Europe. Tracy, overwhelmed with the exciting news interrupted her and said, "I just want to thank you for giving me the opportunity to do this with you guys. It's just amazing."

---

[160] Jeff Pilson interview with James Curl.

Ronnie then spoke up, and with his characteristic frankness said, "Okay, okay, that's cool, but from now on I want you to know, you got this gig because I believe you're equal with us. So don't look at us like we're up here and you're down there. Let's just go in and make a great record and worry about that."[161] It was Ronnie's way of helping Tracy fit in and it worked.

"It gave me lots and lots of confidence hearing the main guy telling me he believed in me," said Tracy. "He knew that I was a little star-struck, because of him. Ronnie Dio's a big name, and he's done a lot of big things."[162]

Following the meeting the guys got busy rehearsing and writing music for a new album. During these first few weeks Tracy got to know Ronnie better. He found that his new roommate was funny and smart and loved spicy curry Indian food, from old imperial Britain. In fact, it was his favorite thing to eat.

Having been introduced to Indian food by Trapeze and Deep Purple singer Glenn Hughes, Ronnie was at first hesitant about trying the strange, spicy cuisine. But once he did he couldn't get enough. And after trying dozens of different recipes, his favorite dish became lamb Vindaloo curry.

It wasn't just European food that Ronnie loved. He was also enamored with the culture, particularly British comedy and was a big fan of Monty Python's Flying Circus, Faulty Towers and The Black Adder.

In addition to British comedy, Ronnie was also a big fan of Mel Blanc, the man behind the voices of such Looney Toons cartoon characters as Bugs Bunny, Daffy Duck, Porky Pig and Yosemite Sam, just to name a few. Ronnie could also mimic several of these cartoon characters nearly as well as Mel. In fact, his answering

---

[161] Ibid.
[162] Ibid.

machine had Ronnie talking just like Yosemite Sam, saying that Ronnie wasn't home.

Tracy also discovered that Ronnie loved animals. He had a cat that came and went as it pleased and a big shaggy dog named Tubbs. Such a lover of animals, Ronnie had taken in numerous rescue animals over the years. Sometime when Ronnie needed a break he and Tracy would take Tubbs for a walk around the neighborhood and toss around song ideas.

Another thing Tracy found out was that Ronnie loved sports. At times he would often write songs while watching the New York Giants, Yankees or the Mets play. While doing so, he would typically enjoy one of his favorite beers like Guinness or some other dark stout.

"I guess I'm the only person who does it that way," said Ronnie. "I could never write songs while listening to music because I couldn't help being influenced by it, and have it take me away from what I want to do."

"Whenever I hear music my mind instantly goes right to music, what it sounds like, how it's produced, what the melody line is like. So, if I listened to music I wouldn't be able to think for myself. The sporting events on TV give me noise, but there's no music to distract me. The noise is from the announcers and from the crowd and I can shut it out when I need to."

"At the same time I'm watching something that I find interesting, something that is part of my fantasy. I always wanted to be an athlete, so I'm speaking from a fantasy world with my music while watching my fantasy on the screen. When I'm preparing for an album, before I do any writing, I'll do a lot of reading. Some science fiction, a lot of historical things, anything that isn't quite real—history obviously was real—but is no more and science fiction is something that will be, but is not yet. I surround myself with this kind of attitude. It makes it easier to spark me into a futuristic or completely ancient frame of mind."

Ronnie's love of sports didn't end with baseball or football. He was also very fond of hockey, basketball and boxing and knew all the records and stats for his favorite fighters and players.

It was during these first few weeks that Jimmy Bain made his exit from the band for personal reasons. Without Jimmy, Ronnie picked up the bass duties for a couple of weeks. Then, one Friday while he Tracy and Vinny were at the studio, Ronnie and Vinny decided to drive over to see their good friend Jeff Pilson.

"One day," said Jeff, "Ronnie and Vinny showed up at my front door. They said that they were practicing down the street and wanted to know if I knew any available bass players and I said, 'Yeah, me!'"

"Great!" replied Ronnie, "Can we go jam?"

Jeff, who had been frantically working in his backyard on leaking lawn sprinklers, said, "Well, I have a problem. My sprinklers are broken and I don't know what to do."

"No problem," replied Ronnie.

"So Ronnie and Vinnie went around to the back of my house and fixed my sprinklers. And then we went down the street and jammed and it was immediate. I knew in my heart the minute they showed up at the door that it was going to be the real deal. Number one, Vinny was one of my best friends at the time, and number two, Ronnie was a dear friend. I'd played with Vinny a lot, he was in my band War and Peace for a long time. We just had a real chemistry, and I knew Ronnie was great. Then when I met Tracy G. it was just immediate. We just started jamming and it was automatic. It was so much fun and the band gelled instantaneously."[163]

Excited with the prospects of the newly formed Dio band, Jeff contacted his band mate Don Dokken. Jeff and Don had been working together for nearly a year writing

---

[163] Ibid.

songs for what would eventually become the *Dysfunctional* album. But at the time, neither was sure what was going to come of their recent collaboration. Jeff broke the news to Don and told him that he was going to join Dio and focus his attention on the newly formed band.

"I had to break the news to Don," said Jeff, "which wasn't fun, but I knew it was the right thing to do. And I'm glad I did because that was a real important lesson for me being in that band."[164]

With Jeff on board, the band spent the next two months writing and rehearsing and another two months tracking and mixing the album. The resulting LP, *Strange Highways*, was different than anything Dio had done before. Gone were the medieval neo-classicisms present in earlier albums like *Holy Diver* and *The Last in Line*. Ronnie's vision for *Strange Highways* was to be more open-minded. He wanted to move beyond the typical fantasy-driven lyrics that were so prevalent on earlier releases. "He wanted to sing more about the world today, and how it was doing," said Tracy. "Things he usually doesn't touch on."[165]

Released on January 26, 1994, *Strange Highways* caught fans off guard with its new progressive sound, one that was heavier than anything Dio had previously released, yet intriguingly contemporary.

The album would arguably turn out to be the darkest and heaviest opus in the Dio catalog and was packed full of mid-tempo, doom metal songs. Moreover, Tracy G's guitar playing was a shock to fans who were expecting a traditional, straight-ahead metal guitarist. Lyrically, the album speaks a lot of negativity and may well be the most pessimistic album Ronnie ever wrote, with themes

---

[164] Ibid.
[165] Interview, Tracy Grijalva with James Curl, December 22, 2016.

dealing with alienation, dysfunctional relationships and disillusionment.

On the positive side, the LP offers up some terrific songs and phenomenal guitar work by the talented and terribly underrated Tracy G. From his heavy riffs to his melodic playing and energetic guitar solos, Tracy shows his versatility and mastery over his instrument. And it's not only Tracy's guitar that stands out, the rhythm section is also outstanding. Pilson's bass playing is fantastic and Vinny's drums are like rolling thunder. Ronnie's mighty pipes are powerful and perhaps more ominous than on any other album. "Ronnie really had to bear down on his voice to sing some of those songs," said Tracy.

Fan reaction to *Strange Highways* was clearly divided; after all, it was a marked departure from what they were accustomed to. Some found the new sound refreshing while others were disappointed. In addition, it didn't help that grunge and rap were the flavor of the day and had the attention of the young. Because of this, *Strange Highways*, like *Lock up the Wolves* and *Dehumanizer,* was easily missed.

The album is, however, a jewel in the Dio catalog that has slowly come to light over the years. "I know Ronnie loved *Strange Highways*," said Pilson, "even though he realized it was a step to the left and might alienate some fans. But he felt that, artistically, it was important to do. I always thought it was an amazing album and was disappointed it didn't come across stronger to fans. Over time, however, I think it's getting recognized and appreciated."[166]

Following the release of the album, Dio headed over to Athens, Greece where they played three shows at the Rodon Club and officially kicked off their world tour.

---

[166] Interview, Jeff Pilson with James Curl, December 23, 2016.

For Tracy, who had never been out of America, the tour was a lot of fun and he was able to take in some tourist attractions. Some of the sites he enjoyed seeing with Ronnie were the Acropolis of Athens, an ancient citadel in Greece and massive, centuries old churches in Spain.

Back in the States the band kicked off the US portion of their tour in Texas on May 1st at the Pecan street festival, a free show. Gone were the days of headlining stadiums, coliseums and huge arenas. Due to lack of ticket sales and the obvious declining interest in heavy metal, Dio was forced to play festivals, clubs and theatres. "This only made the band try that much harder to put on a great show," said Pilson. The tour wrapped up strongly, when Dio headed over to Brazil and played five sold-out shows in a row.

Undeterred by the less than frenzied reception of *Strange Highways* the band went back into the studio and started work on their follow-up album *Angry Machines.*

Following the same direction as *Strange Highways, Angry Machines* was another heavy, angry album, and even more broad-minded than its forerunner. It would in fact become the most progressive album in the Dio collection as well as the most obscure.

Hitting record stores on October 15, 1996 fan response to the album was somewhat more negative than for *Strange Highways.* Most fans felt that Dio had strayed too far from the fundamentals of their original sound while attempting to go into new territories. Even so, the album has, to a smaller degree than *Strange Highways,* slowly come into considerable fan favor over the years. And while many fans still feel that *Angry Machines* marks the lowest point of Dio's career, there are those who have discovered it and think it's little underrated.

"As for *Angry Machines*," said Pilson, "I know Ronnie was excited at the time, but we spoke about it a couple years later and he realized it was too far from fan expectation."[167]

After the release of the album, Dio embarked on a world tour that began in November of 1996 and ran until November of 1997. It was while in Brazil near the end of the tour that Ronnie met Chas West, the lead singer for Bonham. Recalling the first time he met Ronnie, Chas said, "I was in The Jason Bonham Band and we were on tour in South America. I mean, I obviously knew who he was, but we had never personally met."

"It was The Jason Bonham Band, it was Dio, Scorpions and Bruce Dickinson's band and we were the opening band and were playing at a football (soccer) stadium in front of 50,000 people. I'm playing the first night in Sao Paulo, Brazil and the crowd response was great. After the show Ronnie's tour manager comes up to me and says, 'Ronnie would like to meet you; are you gonna be around? Are you gonna hang out?' And I go, 'Yeah, of course.' And he says, 'Okay, stay over here; when we're done you come with me and Ronnie.' He then tells me, 'The band is going to go this way to their dressing room and you come with me and Ronnie this way.' And I said, 'Okay, great' and then I thought to myself, 'Wow.' I mean I couldn't believe what was happening."

"So I stood on the side of the stage and watched the whole show which was phenomenal. And then at the end, exactly as he said, the band went to the right and Ronnie went to the left and the guy looks at me and says, 'Come on, let's go.' Ronnie was carrying a bottle of vodka—Ronnie was drinking vodka tonics on stage and still sang his fucking ass off."

"So we went back and this is a football stadium, so there was just metal lockers and cement floors and

---

[167] Ibid.

wooden benches; there wasn't much there. And I remember we sit down and he pours us both a drink and he pulls out a joint and offers it to me, 'Do you do this?' And I said, 'Well, not normally, but sure why not?' He then says to me, 'The reason you're here is because I was backstage and I heard you singing and I said to my tour manager, who's that kid singing with Bonzo's kid?' Then he complimented me and said, 'Wow, you really got it; you got some pipes.' And I didn't expect that and I was kinda like oh my God. Then he told me, 'I heard you all the way backstage—you blew me away.'"

"And then we just spent time talking for the next two hours. And he gave me advice. He told me what to do and what not to do. He said, 'Don't follow trends; I never did that.' Looking back now, I think he liked me as a person. And he said, 'Sometimes you might have to move on and do other things,' which maybe at that time I wasn't getting. I think maybe he was relating how he had been in Rainbow and how Ritchie had given him his first break and how Jason gave me my first break. I didn't get it at that time. Later on, when the Bonham thing ended, I thought about it and now I understand what he was saying."

"You know he was so gracious and so kind and so giving. Like I said, he spent two hours with me. And he kinda took me under his wing and became my mentor at that point. And he said, 'I'm in L.A.,' and he gave me his number, 'Call me anytime if you need any help, or any advice.' That's the kind of person he was. You know he didn't have to do that; he went out of his way."[168]

Following the *Angry Machines* tour, Dio would not release an album for nearly two-and-a-half years. Instead, Ronnie put out a live album called *Inferno: Last in Live* in '98. From there the band continued to tour the world throughout '98 and '99. They finished the decade on the Monsters of the Millennium tour on November

---

[168] Chas West interview with James Curl.

30, 1999 in the city of Tallinn, in Northern Europe. For Dio it would mark the end of another era.

The 1990s had been a difficult time not only for Dio, but for hard rock and heavy metal in general, particularly in the United States. Grunge and rap had come into their own and snared the attention of America's youth like a hypnotist. Couple that with two albums that most fans had a hard time understanding and Ronnie felt it was time for a change. As a result, by 1999 Ronnie knew that he had to rethink the musical direction of Dio.

Since 1996 the band had been a bit unstable, experiencing multiple lineup changes with drummers and bass players. Sometimes Vinny would be there, sometimes Simon Wright or James Kottack. At other times, Jeff would leave for a time and Larry Denison, Jerry Best or Bob Daisley would fill in on bass. For Ronnie, it was a time to rebuild his foundation and return to heavy metal basics.

"I got a call from Wendy," said Tracy. "'We're going to go to Europe next summer,' she said, 'and play with the Scorpions and do a bunch of outdoor festivals.'" Tracy told Wendy that it sounded like a great idea. She then asked him what he thought of the band bringing on another guitar player to handle the lead guitar spot, while Tracy was relegated to playing rhythm. Tracy's reply was, "No, I wouldn't really be into that." Wendy suggested that Tracy should maybe spend some time and think it over. "I don't have to think about that," was Tracy's reply.

"What's the problem?" asked Tracy.

"Well," said Wendy, "the new record company doesn't want you as the lead guitar player; they don't think you're a good enough lead guitar player and a lot of fans don't understand what you play.'"

"Well, that's okay," replied Tracy. "I'm honored to have had the gig, but I'm not going to bend over backwards and take away my identity, what I've worked my whole life to do just to keep a job."

"Well, I'll call you back in a minute," said Wendy. A moment later Tracy got a call from Ronnie. The two spent about an hour discussing the situation but Tracy held to his conviction, telling Ronnie that, "It sounds like you guys need to go back to Craig Goldy or someone you had before that gives the people more of what they want, what you guys want, what the record company wants."[169]

Ronnie then told Tracy that he would call him back. A few minutes later Ronnie called back and said, "I talked to Wendy and let's just forget it; it was just an idea. Let's just forget that I brought it up and go on with what we have."

"Ok, Ronnie," said Tracy. "Whatever you say."

Hanging up the phone, Tracy knew that his time in Dio was over and figured that he would hear from Ronnie in about a week with more bad news.

As expected, Tracy got a call from Ronnie a week later. Ronnie explained that the only way he could proceed with the new record label was to let Tracy go and get as many of the old members back as he could. Graciously, Tracy accepted his fate, telling Ronnie that if that was what he needed to do to pay the bills then that was okay. The two parted with a mutual respect and a genuine like for each other. Moreover, having played in Dio for nearly seven years Tracy would have the distinct honor of being Dio's longest tenured guitarist.

As for Ronnie, a new concept album would soon be in the works and some old friends would be returning for the next chapter of the Dio epic.

---

[169] Ibid.

Chapter Eleven
Magica, Tenacious D
And Killing the Dragon

With the parting of Tracy G, Ronnie decided to take an old school approach to his next album, while at the same time trying something completely new. Dating as far back as 1987 Ronnie had wanted to do a fantasy-based concept album. For the past several months he had been working on a story, as well as a few songs for a new LP called *Magica*. Speaking of the project Ronnie said,

"When it came to time to do this album I knew that a change was necessary, necessary because I listen to the kids that come to the shows and they keep saying to me: 'We want you to do more things like *Holy Diver*. You haven't done anything like that, you don't tell stories anymore, you don't give us things to think about.'"[170]

Ronnie then went on to say, "Well, I wanted to have a reason to do it, to be truthful. We have been experimenting since the *Dehumanizer* album with Sabbath and onto *Strange Highways* and desperately into *Angry Machines* and the experimental part came in great part because our guitar player was a lot more of an industrial player and not really from the mold of Vivian or from Craig or from Ritchie or those kind of players that I had played with before and, I think, the music got a bit confusing. There were like five years of time where people would speak to us after the show and they would say, 'Oh, well, we like the album' but you could tell that they really didn't like it but they were such great fans and they would say that they did but then they would always

---

[170]*KAOS Magazine*, interview with David Lee Wilson, 2000.

ask, 'Well, are you going to do another *Holy Diver*-style album?'"

Continuing Ronnie said, "When you hear that enough times you realize that really is what they want to hear and perhaps the experimentation had gone a bit too far. I think that was exactly the case and to do this one, there needed to be a reason to do this particular album and it was time. To hearken back to 'olden days' or to *Holy Diver* days or even to Rainbow days, which a lot of this reminds me of, I didn't want people to be able to say, 'Well he couldn't survive in the modern world and he has to do that old album again.' Well, with the concept, there was no other way to do it—nothing else to do but fantasy kind of writing. It is a fantasy concept, therefore the songs needed to be fantasy in nature and it gave me a chance to really sing again."[171]

The idea for *Magica* was dreamt up by Ronnie and is an epic, olden times tale about "good versus evil." Because he wanted it fantasy-based, Ronnie eschewed the modern themes he had sung about on his last two releases. This left him unfettered and free to write about all the medieval things that he loved, something at which he was exceptional.

"*Magica* is the saga of Blessing," said Ronnie, "a netherworld invaded by dark forces that vaporize people into pure, evil energy. The planet's saviors are master apprentice heroes Eriel and Challis, who must recite a spell from the sacred book of *Magica* to defeat their foe, Shadowcast. The album is written from the villain's viewpoint. I took on the evil perspective because I've always written from the anti-perspective. Most people don't think in those terms so you are freer to create. I left the ending ambivalent because evil always exists, good

---

[171] *KAOS Magazine*, interview with David Lee Wilson, 2000.

doesn't always triumph and that's the universal balance."[172]

It was clear at this point that Ronnie felt the time was now right to once again sing about wizards, dragons, and heroes.

Needing a guitarist that could deliver what he wanted, Ronnie contacted Craig Goldy and told him about his idea for the new album, the first of what was intended to be a three-part series. Having worked together previously, Ronnie knew that Craig was capable of playing and writing what he wanted. After discussing some ideas, Craig got excited and agreed to reunite with Dio. He found that Ronnie already had a few songs and about 30 to 40% of the story developed. After hearing the narrative, Craig began thinking about ideas to link the storyline together throughout the songs, like Pink Floyd had done with *Dark Side of the Moon*.

Excited and feeling inspired after getting Craig back in the band, Ronnie then got in touch with his long-time cohort Jimmy Bain. Jimmy had just finished a stint in rehab and part of his ten-step program was to apologize for things he had done while on drugs. So, after the two made amends Ronnie offered to let Jimmy come back on board. It wasn't long after that Vinny decided to jump ship and go play with Black Sabbath. To fill Vinny's spot Ronnie once again recruited the capable Simon Wright, while Scott Warren remained as the stalwart keyboardist.

With a solid foundation built, the boys began working earnestly on the ambitious *Magica*.

"Craig and I helped him a lot with the demos for that album," said Simon. "It took about nine months. We loved watching him create, as he was very excited about the album. I remember him telling me the story behind

---

[172] *"Listen To DIO's: Electra." The Metal Den.com. 19 May 2010. Retrieved 2013-11-13.*

the album and I was very excited and I wondered how it was all going to end up. He created the themes and moods for the songs and it was really amazing. I was helping out creating rough drum machine stuff so we could get from the start to the end of the song. Each song would change and grow. It was a very creative and innovative time."[173]

Although *Magica* harkened back to a more traditional heavy metal sound and style, Ronnie still endeavored to achieve something new and original. And he did! Overall he found that doing the album was easy and enjoyable. "The hardest part," said Ronnie, "was writing the story. Craig and I were on the same page. We worked for about 14 hours a day for about five weeks."[174]

Even though Ronnie was busy with the composition of *Magica* he was also spending whatever free time he could spare volunteering with the Children of the Night Foundation. The non-profit charity was founded in 1979 by Dr. Louis Lee with the goal of getting adolescent runaways, sexually abused children and prostitutes off the streets of Los Angeles and help them to re-enter mainstream society.

Ronnie had been involved with the organization for about ten years and found the work rewarding. Even some of his fellow musicians like Ozzy Osbourne and Richard Marx got involved. Speaking of Ronnie's contributions and unselfish work, Dr. Lois Lee said,

"Ronnie was very generous to Children of the Night with his time and money. He led rock 'n' roll to help build a home for America's child prostitutes before the word 'sex-trafficking' was invented. He shared my

---

[173] Simon Wright a Disciple of Dio, by Jeb Wright, Classic Rock Revisited.
[174] You Tube interview, Robbs Metal Works 2000.

vision to make the world a better place for children who had nowhere else to turn for help."[175]

Speaking of the charity Ronnie said, "I think charity work is important, but the best kind of giving you can ever give is anonymous because you're doing it for yourself. There's no way on earth that anybody could consider that you're doing it for anything, but yourself. Unfortunately, I'm going to have to be at the head of a lot of this. So, I'm going to get a lot of the accolades or shit. I can't give anonymously, but a lot of other people do and I think it's important. It's important to care about mankind especially kids. I mean, Good Lord, give me a break. It's a charity that primarily deals with sexually abused kids. What these kids are going through is horrible. They just die. I know them then they're gone. It's just terrible."

"We should all do something. We try to get them off the street, if not, to save them forever, at least give them a modicum of a life that is certainly a whole lot better. You've gotta be a human being first 'cause that's what we all are. We just have different labels, 'Oh, man! He sings great! Wow, he writes great!' Labels are something they have to put on us, but we don't have to believe them."[176]

At one point, there were even talks of doing a project similar to Hear 'n Aid, but unfortunately Ronnie never found the time. He did however manage to play a couple of charity concerts in the early '90s that benefited the foundation.

Despite a hectic schedule Ronnie succeeded in getting *Magica* completed. The album was released on March

---

[175] Dr. Lois Lee, interview with James Curl.
[176] Rock Confidential, Exclusive Interview: Ronnie James Dio, by Jesse Capps, November 21, 2004.

21, 2000 and was seen as his most inspired work in years. Moreover, it was also far different than anything he had done during the Tracy G. era.

From the start the album received a lot of positive praise from fans and critics alike. Like some ancient sorcerer, Ronnie had woven his spell and alchemized the songs together with an expert hand. As a whole the album is cohesive and the songs flow together smoothly. Ronnie even experimented a little with different sound effects and music. An example of this can be heard on the song "Losing My Insanity" which has a folky element that gives one the impression they're at a Middle Ages festival.

Another song that stands out, at least in the opening segment, is "As Long As It's Not About Love." The song highlights Ronnie's vocal versatility and shows that at 58-years of age his voice had exhibited little signs of aging or slowing down. As a bonus, at the end of the LP Ronnie narrates an 18-minute telling of the *Magica* story that is well-done and makes what is a somewhat typical fantasy story really come to life.

By the time Ronnie was writing *Magica* in 1999 he had become a full-fledged heavy metal icon. Such was his popularity that it had begun to transcend the boundaries of music. One example of this was when Ronnie was featured on the animated sitcom, South Park. The wildly popular show was well-known for its mocking and hilarious parodies of celebrities and famous musicians; in fact, several of Ronnie's contemporaries had already been featured.

Knowing full well the show's reputation, Ronnie was at first understandably hesitant. "Initially," said Ronnie, "I didn't want to let it be done because I felt that they were just going to crucify me and that I would end up being like what they did to Rod Stewart and what they did to Elton John and what they did to Ozzy." But, after giving it some thought Ronnie relented, saying, "So I thought to myself, 'Well, if you want to be an American icon, you better let them do it.'"[177]

In one particular interview Ronnie explains how the South Park episode came to be. "Well, South Park was very strange. I got a call from Wendy, my manager, who said, 'I just got a call from South Park and they want to use "Holy Diver"' I said, 'Get the fuck out; they'll crucify me.' She said, 'No, they're really big Dio fans.' I said, 'Sure. I'm sure that's going to work.' She said, 'No, I'm telling you they are.' So, I thought to myself, no matter what they do to me, this is an opportunity to make me part of Americana. I let that one go."

"How many people could be part of South Park? I said, 'Go for it.' They did it. I saw it and thought it was great. They gave me more attention than they ever gave anybody else, certainly musically. They played the whole song and they played it on the credits of the outset. In fact, somebody from Warner Bros., where we used to be signed, called up, because we stay in close contact, called up and said, 'We've never seen treatment like that. They must've loved you.' It was great. Even if they crucified me, I felt that I could've dealt with it. I think that what made me most proud of it all was that the people who did it kind of knew that I'm not an asshole and so they didn't treat me like an asshole. That, to me, was the most precious thing about it all. It's one of the funniest ones I've seen. It really was great."[178]

The accolades didn't end with South Park. In 2001 the band Tenacious D, featuring actor Jack Black and his

---

[177] *Dio, Ronnie James (2002). "Reality Check TV, episode #291."* Reality Check TV (Interview). Interview with Danny Shipman.

[178] *KAOS magazine,* interview Ronnie James Dio, March 27, 2000.

band mate Kyle Gass, paid homage to Ronnie by writing a song about the iconic singer.

Jack and Kyle had formed Tenacious D back in 1994 and were huge fans of Ronnie. Remembering the first time he became aware of Ronnie, Jack said: "The first time I heard of Ronnie James Dio was the summer of 1982. I was 13-years-old, living in Culver City, California. A kid across the street was wearing this kick-ass *Mob Rules* baseball T-shirt. It had an ominous painting of some faceless creatures holding whips. I bought the album and was blown away by the title track right out of the gate. Dio's gymnastic vocalizations along with guitarist Tony Iommi's rolling thunder riffs were impossible to resist. This was my introduction to Black Sabbath and set the stage for my lifelong obsession with heavy metal music."[179]

Although Jack and Kyle are both serious musicians, their music has a strong comedic element that "fuses vulgar lyrics and absurdist comedy with rock music." Their unique style has been described by critics as "mock rock." As one might imagine from a band like Tenacious D, the song they wrote about Ronnie is very tongue in cheek. And although it was done to honor Ronnie, it also requested that he "pass the torch" and essentially retire because he has rocked for a long time. The track, simply titled "Dio," was released on their platinum-selling debut album in September of 2001 and goes like this,

"Dio has rocked for a long, long time.
Now it's time for him to pass the torch.
He has songs of wildebeests and angels.
He has soared on the wings of a demon.
It's time to pass the torch.
You're too old to rock, no more rockin' for you.
We're takin' you to a home.

---

[179] Jack Black remembers Ronnie James Dio: "He Kicked Major Ass," *Rolling Stone Magazine*, By Kory Grow, May 15, 2015.

But we will sing a song about you.
And we will make sure that you're very well taken care of.
You'll tell us secrets that you've learned.
Raow!
Your sauce will mix with ours,
and we'll make a good goulash baby.
Dio, time to go!"

At first it might seem that Ronnie would have taken offense to the song, but after hearing it he thought it was funny. He then went on to say that he had no intention of "passing the torch."

"We had no idea how he would react to the song," said Jack. "It was about how we wanted him to pass the torch of rock supremacy to us, Tenacious D, and that he'd enjoyed the spoils of heavy metal dominance long enough and it was our turn to reign supreme. Ultimately, it was an ode to his greatness but it could've easily been misconstrued as an insult. But Dio was a wise soul. He felt the love behind our humor and put our minds at ease. It was something he was known for: When he wasn't onstage raising hell, he exuded a mellow peaceful vibe. His hang-ability quotient was extremely high."[180]

With *Magica* and a subsequent world tour behind him Ronnie began working on a follow-up in 2001 titled *Killing the Dragon*. Although Craig was there for much of the early work on the new LP, he had other pressing matters that required his attention. At home his wife was pregnant and he was also busy working a day job. With so many other responsibilities to handle, he wasn't able to focus 100% of his attention on the band, so he decided to leave.

To replace Craig, Ronnie brought in the sensationally gifted guitarist, Doug Aldrich who had been playing with

---

[180] Jack Black remembers Ronnie James Dio: "He Kicked Major Ass," *Rolling Stone Magazine*, By Kory Grow, May 15, 2015.

Lion and Black Rain. Like most great guitarists, Doug was first introduced to the guitar as a youngster; in his case he began playing at 11. His first guitar was a Les Paul purchased from Sears and from then on he was rarely without it.

Years later Doug auditioned for Kiss, but didn't get the gig. He did however become friends with Gene Simmons and he and Gene remain friends to this day. Besides playing music, Doug was also a highly sought-after guitar teacher, and at one point he was teaching over 70 students a week.

With Doug on board and *Magica* being a success, Ronnie continued to stick with what he knew best; writing a straight ahead rock 'n' roll record. With a majority of the songs written before Craig left, Ronnie, Doug and Jimmy got busy coming up with a couple more tracks needed to complete the album. Remembering the time, Doug said, "It was a strange experience because I had come in after most of the stuff had been written." Nevertheless, Doug meshed well with the guys and in no time, they had the last few songs completed.

During an interview on the TV show Uranium, Ronnie talks about the upcoming album and explains that the "Dragon" of the album title is metaphorical and refers to modern technology. He then expressed his concern with it threatening society in the future.

He went on to explain that the title track refers to "those who perpetrate injustices and what the world is doing to stop them. In fantasy tales, dragons were notorious for stealing children and feeding them to their babies. During the first part of the song, I sing 'Someone has taken a child.' The second part is about a cruel feudal lord. The third part is about 'electronic serfdom.'" Ronnie then went on to express his belief that the computer has become a god in modern-day society. "It is a small god with an electrical heart. It is time to rebel against it."[181]

Released May 21, 2002 *Killing the Dragon* is unabashedly Dio and even more of a conventional rock album and return to old school form than *Magica*. Although at times it relies on the symbolic and medieval imagery and lyrics that Ronnie loved to use, he does sing about modern themes. The song "Throw Away Children" for example is about runaway kids. Moreover, it was slated to be used for a sequel to Hear 'n Aid to raise money for the Children of the Night. The song however was thought to be a little too depressing. According to Ronnie the foundation wanted something a little more upbeat and "anthem-y."

In a way the album is a throw-back and reminiscent of *Dream Evil* and *Sacred Heart,* and overall delivers some excellent songs. The opening track "Killing the Dragon," is "a rip-snorter of a galloping metal anthem that was arguably Ronnie's most impressive riff rocker in years,"[182] says music journalist Martin Popoff.

From the album came the melodic and upbeat hit single "Push." When the time came to film a video for the song, Ronnie thought it might be fun to have Jack and Kyle make a cameo. Since the two were friends with one of the directors of Ronnie's record company it was easy for Ronnie to get in touch with the pair.

Told what Ronnie wanted to do, the Tenacious D boys were excited and eagerly accepted. Talking about meeting his hero on the set of the video, Jack said, "We did get to meet him, me and Kyle. We sang a song about Dio on a Tenacious D album and he heard about it and he reached out and he said, 'Hey, do you guys wanna be

---

[181] Wikipedia: *Killing the Dragon.*
[182] Dio: light beyond the black, by Martin Popoff, *Metal Blade Records*, 2006, pg 169.

in a music video?' So we did a little cameo in one of his music videos and it was a thrill."[183] "We were nervous to meet him, but he couldn't have been a nicer guy. He was super warm and jovial, humble and relaxed—a real class act with a tremendous sense of humor."[184]

While filming the video the three became fast friends and had a lot of fun working together. It wouldn't be the last time the trio would cross paths.

---

[183] Planet Rock: Jack Black explains why Ronnie James Dio is his favorite heavy metal singer ever, by Scott Colothan, Friday December 15, 2017.
[184] Jack Black remembers Ronnie James Dio: "He Kicked Major Ass," *Rolling Stone Magazine,* By Kory Grow, May 15, 2015.

Chapter Twelve
Master of the Moon, and the Pick of Destiny

After releasing *Killing the Dragon*, Dio embarked on a world tour that ran from May 2002 until August of 2003. Following the tour Ronnie was kept busy with domestic things. He and Wendy owned an antique store called the Ivy Cottage as well as a limousine service; both businesses required a lot of attention. Luckily for Ronnie, Wendy handled the majority of the responsibilities. This allowed Ronnie time to work on a new album and spend time gardening and working in his back yard, which was one of his favorite past-times.

While gardening on one particular occasion Ronnie severed the end of his thumb off and thought his days of flashing his devil horns were over for good.

"It was a killer garden gnome," said Ronnie. "I'm not joking, although I certainly wish I was. What happened was that I was in my yard trying to place this garden gnome on a slope. This is a seriously heavy piece of garden ornament, probably 60 pounds or so. Anyway, it fell over, I fell into the shrubbery and then began to slide down to the bottom of the hill. I was trying to stop myself with my feet but put my hand out at the wrong moment. You can understand this all happened in a split second. My hand landed on a rock, and the gnome landed on it, squashing my thumb between the rock and the gnome. Basically it was crushed and took the end of my thumb off. I just looked at my hand and the first thought that flashed into my mind was, 'How on earth am I going to make my devil horn sign now? That's my trademark!' I wasn't worried about the injury, more concerned with my career."

Continuing he said, "I just picked up the end of the thumb, went back into the house, washed the nub of my thumb then got myself down to the hospital. It was quite surreal because I had one hand with this crushed thumb, basically just red meat and miniscule bits of bone, and I was holding the end of the thumb in my other hand. It was quite fascinating. It's not too often you get to see inside your thumb. I got a shock when I arrived in the emergency room because a nurse took a look at it first and said, 'No, I don't think we can save this.' I had to wait a while then for a doctor, all the time praying that he would come up with a different evaluation. Anyhow, he did thankfully. He said he could sew it back on. 'Please do!' I said, and that's exactly what he did."[185]

Ronnie's hairdresser Joey recalls a time he experienced Ronnie and Simon building a concrete wall in the back yard. "One day," says Joey, "I was at Ronnie's place and he says, 'Hey, Joey, come with us, we gotta make a run.' I said, 'Where we going?' and he said, 'Home Depot.' So, I'm in Home Depot with Ronnie and Simon and they're dressed in overalls and their hair is all messed up and there's concrete all over their faces and they're buying cement. And nobody knows who they are; they just think Ronnie is some old guy with long hair."[186]

Around this time Ronnie was also involved in a number of interesting interviews. One in particular dealt with religion and his personal views on the subject. The interview was done by musician and filmmaker Sam Dunn at Ronnie's home. Sam was in the process of filming a documentary called *Metal: A Head Banger's Journey* and had already interviewed a number of

---

[185] Blabbermouth.net, Ronnie James Dio talks about being attacked by a killer gnome, September 10, 2003.
[186] Joey Belfiore interview with James Curl.

legendary rockers like Lemmy, Tony Iommi and Bruce Dickinson.

While the goal of the documentary was to get people's opinions and discuss the origins, culture and controversy that often surrounds heavy metal, for this interview Sam and Ronnie focused on religion and Satanism.

Right or wrong, since its inception, heavy metal has been controversial and has been associated with the Devil and Satanism. Many bands throughout the history of rock 'n' roll have been labeled "Satanic" and Dio was no different. With the highly provocative *Holy Diver* album cover, that showed a priest being drowned by a demon-like being, it's easy to see how Dio was tagged with such a strong label.

Ronnie however was not a Satanist, in fact his religious point of view was probably not what one would expect from a person who grew up in a strict Catholic Italian home. When asked by Sam to explain how religion had played a part in his music, Ronnie responded with his characteristic honesty, saying, "Religion has played a part in my music more from a dissatisfaction, a discontented view. I believe that any religion is a great religion because it gives people the strength, some people, the strength to go on—they have to have faith. And they believe that the ultimate goal of reaching nirvana or heaven is because there'll be good people. Hey, you can't ask for more than that. That's great, religion should be teaching love and it should be teaching that there is something probably higher than we are out there to lessen our sense of importance."

"So as far as religion goes, I've always dealt with it that way that it's a good thing, but I think maybe sometimes the teachings don't hold true to themselves—thou shall not kill, an eye for an eye, no I don't think so. So that's why for me the whole world is heaven and hell. That song is about that, the fact that, in my mind we live in heaven and we live in hell. God and the Devil are inherent in each of us; it's our choice to make. You can take the road to good or you can take the road to bad; well we have a choice. The optimum way to go of course is to do the good thing."[187]

In a separate interview Ronnie spoke of his religious beliefs further, saying, "I don't believe in either heaven or hell as a place to go to when we die, that you know, when we die we're gonna go down and burn for a while and if we're good we're gonna go up there and be happy for a while, or purgatory where all the little unbaptized babies are hanging out. I think anybody that has that kind of idea that there's a place where little children are going to be hanging out for the rest of their lives is either the sickest person on earth or the stupidest person on earth— I think both of those things apply."

"So I don't believe in any of those things. My belief in heaven and hell is heaven and hell is right here, this is where we are, this is heaven, this is hell. You make your own heaven, you make your own hell. Good and evil, God and the Devil reside in each of us. I don't need to go to a place to pray, I can pray inside myself. I can pray to whomever I want to inside myself and get the same results. I don't need to be told by a priest that I'm bad. Or to be told by a nun that I'm not learning my project properly and get smacked on the head with a ruler. Who the hell are you to do that to me? Or to be told here's God and God has been nailed to a piece of wood; it's not the way I want to think of life, I don't think of it that way."

"And with all the religions that there are preaching all the same things, it's really one great big homogenized thing anyway. At the end of the day if we all just believe in the same thing, you know that we have a choice between good and evil, make your choice, that's all it's about to me."[188]

---

[187] Chris Dunn interview with Ronnie James Dio, *Metal: A Headbanger's Journey* documentary 2004.
[188] You Tube interview, Ronnie James Dio talks religion.

In yet another interview Ronnie did for Heavy Metal magazine, the singer was asked what he thought about Jesus Christ. "I think that He was a prophet," answered Ronnie. "I've had a difficult time coming to terms with Jesus Christ as the Son of God. He was a great man for the time... The thing that bothers me about taking that conclusion is that most of the general statements that Christ made, you can look at the dead language of Greek at the time it was used, and the writing styles that shifted around 50 A.D., you can pretty much date parts of the New Testament. Then His whole claim to be the only way wouldn't make Him a good prophet, because like a lot of Muslims believe that Jesus was a great prophet in the lineage of prophets. But a good prophet is not gonna stand up there and say, 'I'm the only way to the Father.' He's either a liar or He's a crazy man."[189]

When asked about the Bible in one particular interview Ronnie said he "felt that the Bible was only a book of such ancient origin that has been changed from time immemorial so that it becomes not even close to what, if those people actually wrote it, you know what I mean? It's crap. Come on. I tell you a story, you tell 15 other people, and by the end of the day it becomes something else. I don't believe in it."

Despite interviews and a schedule that kept him on his toes, Ronnie found time to work on a new album. Early on he intended to write *Magica II* and *III*, however as work progressed, time became an issue so he decided to wait on continuing the *Magica* saga. Instead the new LP became a "songs" album titled *Master of the Moon.*

Although Jimmy was around for much of the early writing he eventually decided to quit and regroup with Vinny Appice and the band World War III. Rumors however swirled that he had fallen off the wagon after being clean for a few years and his interest in the band

---

[189] *Heavy Metal Magazine*, The Catholic Struggles of Ronnie James Dio.

had waned. Shortly after quitting, Jimmy posted on the Dio message board saying, "My heart wasn't in it. When your heart isn't in it you can't really do it anymore. I want to do something where maybe I can get rich as opposed to other people getting rich and I didn't. That is unfortunate but such is life. When you join a band you think that everything is going to be great and it doesn't end up like that so you have to leave after such a long time."

By this time Doug was also gone, having signed up to play with Whitesnake. His departure however wasn't without some regret. "Unfortunately, we didn't get to pursue the chemistry Ronnie and I had," said Doug about departing from Dio. "But maybe in the future we'll get a chance to write some more stuff."

Needing to repopulate the band, Ronnie once again reunited with long-time friends Jeff Pilson and Craig Goldy. Getting those two back in the band was an easy transition for Ronnie and work on the album progressed rapidly. The rest of the band remained the same with the ever loyal Scott and Simon sticking to their respective positions.

By September 7, 2004 Dio was ready with a new album. Unfortunately it would be the last one the band would ever put out. Not in the mood to write about medieval fantasy, Ronnie wrote much of the album with themes and lyrics that reflected real world relevance.

Speaking of the album Ronnie said, "I think it is a product of the time, really. We actually started with the thought of writing the next two parts of *Magica*. We were in that mind-set right away and then I realized there wasn't going to be enough time to do that properly so we embarked upon the album you hear now."

"Because we were in that mind-set I think a lot of this album became a lot more realistic, touching upon events that are happening in the world today. It turned out to be the heaviest of the Dio productions so far, as far as sound-wise goes. I think some of that had to do with the fact that we thought we were going to do *Magica*, which would have been a bigger, broader piece. The things that were happening at that time are the same things that are happening now—terrorism, the war in Iraq—I could go on and on about all the horrible things that are going on in this world. I really couldn't bring myself to write a whole lot of things about fantasy when all you hear about is real death and destruction."[190]

"*Master of the Moon* is one of those albums the fans are either going to like or dislike," said Ronnie. Right from the start the listener will notice the meaty production and full sound. For the fans who liked *Strange Highways* and *Magica*, as well as heavy, doom metal-type songs, the album certainly delivers.

Compared to *Killing the Dragon*, the music is slower, darker and heavier and filled with crunching riffs. The album does however offer some welcome variety with faster tracks like "One More for the Road" and "Living the Lie." In addition there are a few mid-tempo songs mixed in as well. Overall, the album ends the Dio catalog on a positive note, and like *Strange Highways* is slowly becoming more appreciated as the years go by.

To support the album, Dio set out on a world tour, but not before adding a new member. Jeff who was about to become a father for the first time was unable to get away. "Ronnie knew up front that I wouldn't be able to tour," said Jeff. "We were about to have our daughter and he was cool with that and he endorsed the idea of us starting a family."

For Jeff it would be the last time he would work with Ronnie, however his two stints in the band are remembered fondly. "Ronnie was really soulful, just a really soulful human being," reflects Jeff. "Really fiery and passionate which meant he could get really angry. Although I have to say he never got angry with me; that

---

[190] Rock Confidential, Exclusive Interview: Ronnie James Dio, by Jesse Capps, November 21, 2004.

was a nice benefit for me. But I did see him get angry with people and it was brutal, he could be brutal. But at the same time he was very respectful and he was very loving. So even if he was angry or whatever it never felt out of line. He would turn around and then give these people the biggest hugs in the world."

"He was just a passionate guy. He was high energy in a certain way that was unbeatable. He had a certain energy; you just couldn't top it. So yeah, I mean passionate, fiery, really soulful, really loving, caring. He knew all about your life. He took the time to really know people and it wasn't just surface stuff. You know, most people say, 'How ya doing?' and you know they really don't care because that's what you're supposed to ask. But he did care; he really did care. When he would ask, 'How ya doing?' he would listen. As a result he was a really tremendous friend. I went through some dark periods that he was right there for me and I'll never forget that."[191]

To replace Jeff, Ronnie hired the revered journeyman Rudy Sarzo of Quiet Riot, Ozzy and Whitesnake fame. From there Dio headed over to Moscow, Russia in July of '04 to start their run.

In 2005 while in the midst of the *Masters of the Moon* tour, Ronnie was offered a chance to once again work with the boys from Tenacious D. Jack and Kyle were filming a movie called *The Pick of Destiny* and wanted Ronnie to make an appearance.

"I got a call," said Ronnie, "and Jack said, 'We're doing the film and I want you to play the part of Ronnie James Dio! And if you don't, I'm not going to make the film.' Then he added on to it, 'Well, maybe we will, but it won't be as good without you.' So, that was really interesting for me. So, I did that for Jack. He did me a turn, I did him one and it was really interesting. It's my first film but to me it was like a giant video. Not that

---

[191] Jeff Pilson interview with James Curl.

much different than any of the other videos I'd done because it was more of a performance piece for me."[192]

The movie is a fantasy comedy about a young boy named JB (Jack) who leaves his oppressive religious family and heads for Hollywood on a quest to form the world's most awesome rock band. JB is sent on the quest while praying to a poster of Dio for guidance. Ronnie, who is seated on a skull-tipped throne suddenly comes to life much to the surprise of the boy and tells JB what he must do to fulfill his rock 'n' roll destiny, all the while singing "an epic rock opera." Speaking of the scene, Ronnie says, "The kid's sitting on the bed and he starts to sing to a huge poster of me. He's asking me what to do, saying all he really wants to do is rock 'n' roll. Then I come alive from the poster and tell him, "Go to Hollywood where you'll meet your partner and rock 'n' roll forever."[193]

Talking about the movie during an interview, Jack explained how Ronnie became involved with the film.

"After establishing a relationship with him," said Jack, "we were emboldened to ask a favor of our new friend. He agreed to perform a cameo in our movie. It was for the opening song in the film and required a pre-recording studio visit. He showed up like a seasoned vet all warmed-up and ready to blow doors down. I swear he nailed it on the first take. He offered to double the vocal but we wouldn't hear of it. Those pipes were pristine and required no bolstering whatsoever."[194]

Jack went on to say, "I was embarrassed because the song we wrote borrowed heavily from a song he wrote years before, [Black Sabbath's] "Neon Knights," but while he recognized the similarities he graciously placed it in the category of an 'homage' and gave us his full

---

[192] Rock Eyes, interview with Ronnie James Dio,
[193] Blabbermouth, Ronnie James Dio discusses appearance in "the Pick of Destiny" movie, by Chris Lee, October 15, 2006.
[194] Jack Black remembers Ronnie James Dio: "He Kicked Major Ass," *Rolling Stone Magazine*, By Kory Grow, May 15, 2015.

blessing. He also gave a blistering acting performance on film and I really can't imagine the movie without him. He was actually too good—by far, the best part of the movie. Look at how many downloads his scene has on YouTube. He's a tough act to follow indeed!"

Hitting the theatres in 2006, *The Pick of Destiny* was a box office bomb, however Ronnie's performance was a highlight that most metal fans found enjoyable.

It wasn't just interviews and a movie that Ronnie was involved with during 2005; he also participated in the Queensrÿche concept album *Operation: Mindcrime II*. Ronnie's role was that of Dr. X, a manipulative demagogue.

Vocalist Geoff Tate, who was a big fan of Ronnie's, was excited to have him involved saying, "Ronnie was very, I would say, inspirational and instrumental in my career. He was the first major act to invite us on a tour of Europe. And we spent two, two-and-a-half months touring Europe with him. We played so many shows together. And he was really a great mentor—friendly. He was just such a unique, giving, responsible, friendly, good person."[195]

Throughout the recording process Geoff kept the identity of Dr. X a secret until the album was completed. He then officially announced that Ronnie was indeed the voice of the notorious villain. Speaking of being chosen to play the part, Ronnie said, "I was flattered to be asked to be part of the *Operation: Mindcrime II* project, and it was truly great to work with Geoff Tate again."[196]

Not only did Ronnie record on the album, but he also participated in dozens of live shows as a "special guest." For the fans it was a welcome bonus. Speaking about it, Ronnie said, "I've been asked to reprise my performance

---

[195] Blabbermouth, Geoff Tate Remembers Ronnie James Dio: "He was such a unique, giving, responsible, friendly, good person." December 30, 2016.
[196] KNAC.com, Queensrÿche villain Dr. X unmasked, by Diana DeVille, Rock Goddess, December 16, 2005.

as Dr. X on *Operation: Mindcrime II* in a live venue. It worked out where I was able to do it for this show, and it should be quite a treat."[197]

Having completed *Operation: Mindcrime II* Ronnie resumed the *Masters of the Moon* tour. On June 1, 2006 while he was in Stuttgart, Germany his mother Anna passed away. Anna had been sick for some time and Ronnie had been making frequent trips to Cortland whenever he could. Having been close with her, he was devastated by her passing.

In December of 2006 Ronnie wrapped up the *Masters of the Moon* tour. With hardly any time to rest he was back at work with a new project. Three months earlier, in September, Tony Iommi had reached out to Ronnie informing him that the record company wanted to release a compilation of Dio-era Black Sabbath music. Tony also wanted to know if Ronnie would be interested in writing two new songs specifically for the release. Having always written well with Tony, Ronnie agreed to get involved and a new project was unwittingly born.

---

[197] KNAC.com, Queensrÿche villain Dr. X unmasked, by Diana DeVille, Rock Goddess, August 17, 2006.

Chapter Thirteen
Heaven & Hell

Having agreed to work with Tony on a couple of songs, Ronnie flew over to England where the two met up. Back at Tony's place they sipped strong coffee and visited for a while. The two friends had only seen each other one other time in nearly 15-years, at a recent gig in Birmingham, so it took a while to get reacquainted.

After catching up they went into Tony's studio and got to work. It was quickly evident that the chemistry they had shared years before was still as strong as ever. They were in fact so inspired that instead of coming up with two songs, like the record company wanted, they came up with three.

The first song they wrote was a slow one called "Shadow of the Wind." Tony then came up with a riff for a mid-tempo song that would eventually become "The Devil Cried." A few days later Ronnie returned to Los Angeles. The two continued to collaborate and write, albeit long distance, and eventually came up with a fast song called "Ear in the Wall."

A few weeks later Ronnie was back at Tony's place along with Geezer Butler and Bill Ward. Tony had demoed the new songs for his band mates and Geezer really liked what he heard. Bill, however was a little more critical. After hearing the songs he wanted to examine and try different things with each one.

After a few days of playing with them he eventually came to the conclusion that he really wasn't happy with the tracks. The four then discussed touring again. Ronnie, Tony and Geezer were all for it, but Bill wasn't particularly keen on the idea of getting back on the road. In the end the three decided to go on without him and agreed to give Vinny a call.

Getting Vinny back in the band would make perfect sense, especially since he was familiar with the songs they would be playing. Bill on the other hand would have to learn the majority of the set list which would be from *Dehumanizer* and *Mob Rules*, albums that Vinny had played on.

A few days later Vinny got a call from Wendy. She told him that Ronnie, Tony and Geezer were thinking of touring and wanted him back in the band. It was then that Vinny decided to play a prank.

"When Heaven & Hell got together in 2006," said Vinny, "Wendy Dio called me up and said, 'Hey, look, it's not working with Bill Ward. We want you to come out and play on the album and band, come to England' and stuff. So I made a deal with her. I hadn't really spoken to Wendy in four or five years. Ronnie and I spoke here and there, but we didn't really see each other."

"So I told Wendy after the deal was made, 'I've gotta tell you something.' She goes, 'What?' I said, 'I gained a whole bunch of weight. I'm almost 300 pounds.' She goes, 'What?' And I said, 'I've gotta get an extra-heavy stool made for me.' But she already made the deal, so what are you gonna do? And I left it at that, and I flew over to England. So everybody's thinking I'm, like, 300 pounds, probably can't play as good as I did. And when I got there, the next day I went to Tony's house—that's where they were, at his studio—when I got there, they said, 'Vinny's here,' and they were all peeking around the corner to see what I looked like. And then I walked in, and they go, 'You bastard! You lying…' It was great. It was awesome. But that broke the ice of not seeing everybody instantly."[198]

With Vinny back in the band, the guys completed the three tracks and began rehearsing for the inevitable tour that would follow. As expected, as soon as word got out

---

[198] Blabbermouth, Vinny Appice recalls pranking Heaven and Hell bandmates, November 27, 2017.

that Ronnie and Tony had completed three new songs, promoters began calling and asking when they were going to tour. Following some discussions the guys decided to take it slow. They didn't want to commit themselves for an extended outing that might last years.

By March of 2007 a full-fledged tour was booked to support the release of Black Sabbath: *The Dio Years*. The guys headed out to Canada to begin the tour but not as Black Sabbath. Wanting something new and fresh they decided on the name Heaven & Hell. Everyone was already referring to them as Heaven & Hell and it was a name that fit perfectly. Moreover, it was less confusing and distinguished them from Black Sabbath, who had recently been touring with Ozzy.

After playing 11 shows across Canada, Heaven & Hell headed to New York to play at the Radio City Music Hall. Following the show Ronnie made a trip to Cortland where he met up with his cousin Dave Feinstein. The two had been talking about doing a project together for some time and now that Ronnie had a three-week break between shows they decided to make it happen.

Speaking of the project, Dave said, "For years Ronnie and I talked about doing some music project together, like an Elf reunion or a guest appearance on a Rods album or a solo album. We wanted to do something, but he lived 3,000 miles away from me, so that made it a bit difficult. He also had a very busy schedule. But when we would see each other, we would always talk about it. In my mind, I always wanted to do something and he did too. And then a couple years ago, his mother became ill, so he was coming back home pretty frequently. I got a call one day and he said he was going be in town for a few days and he would be able to sing a couple of songs. Coincidentally, I had just written "Metal Will Never Die" the day before he called. Carl (Canedy, drummer of the Rods) and I were in the process of putting together a new Rods record."

"So, the next day I got together with Carl and told him that Ronnie was coming over, so we need to pick out a couple songs that he can sing on. But before we did that I wanted to make a demo of the song that I just wrote because I didn't have it down on tape yet and I didn't want to forget it. So we put together a demo version and when we finished it, I said this is one of the songs that Ronnie has got to sing. It would be perfect for him."

"So we chose that song and another one, which will be on the next Rods record. The next day, I picked Ronnie and Wendy up at the airport and gave him a CD of two songs that he had never heard before. We didn't listen to them on that night, because he just flew in. We just socialized and had a few beers. But then the next day, we came into the studio and he put the songs into a boom box and listened for a bit, and then did a world class performance on both of the songs. It was unbelievable, but that was the way that Ronnie worked. I was exposed to that in working with him before, but Carl hadn't. And Carl couldn't believe that Ronnie could just go in and nail it right away. Ronnie also had a unique talent of knowing exactly what a song needed. And that's what he did with 'Metal Will Never Die.'"[199]

"Metal Will Never Die" would eventually be released in 2010 on Feinstein's solo album *Bitten by the Beast*. The other song "The Code," would come out a year later on the Rods' *Vengeance* album.

Remembering the experience of recording with Ronnie, Carl said, "It was pretty amazing. David always talked about Ronnie being this 'one take guy.' You would always hear about it and hear people talk about it. You know, the longer you are away from something the more you glorify it, the more you think of it as being totally perfect and just amazing and maybe being more amazing than it once was. But in this case Ronnie came

---

[199] BraveWorlds, Dave rock Feinstein on recording Metal Will Never Die with Ronnie James Dio, November 14, 2010.

in very humble and sang. It was just unbelievable and it truly was 'one take.'"

"The only time he did anything again was to try something different and that was only a couple of little things. But he never redid anything because of a take, not one time; both songs he just nailed them... incredible. And I worked with so many great singers, that to see that, it was everything David said it was. I just didn't think that those kind of phenomenal singers were out there, that that was something that people could actually do, but that was Ronnie; he really was that 'one take guy' just like David said."[200]

After Ronnie finished up in Cortland, he regrouped with his band mates. Heaven & Hell resumed their tour of America then headed over to Europe in June for some summer festivals and arena shows.

By September they were back in America playing 20 shows with Alice Cooper and Queensrÿche. The guys then made a short run through Japan in late October. It was during this time, as the tour was nearing its finale, that the guys were feeling a bit crestfallen and thinking this might be the end. Because the tour had been so much fun and successful, Tony approached Ronnie about doing another album, to which Ronnie replied, "Yeah, I'd love to do that."

The two then brought up the idea to Geezer and Vinny, who were both willing to keep a good thing going. With plans for a new album and having finished in Japan, the guys headed over to the UK where they wrapped up touring in November of 2007.

A couple of months later everyone met up at Ronnie's place. For the past few months each member had done some recordings on CDs and now that they were together, they went over what they had. Initially there were about 20 song ideas. Over some drinks in Ronnie's

---

[200] Carl Cannedy interview with James Curl.

studio they picked out the ones they liked best and spent the next few days working the songs over.

One of the first songs that they completed was a song that Ronnie had come up with called "Atom and Evil." Ronnie had written the lyrics and music and everyone thought it was terrific. Eventually it would become the first song on the album.

After a short break to do the Metal Masters tour that ran through August of 2008 the guys got back to work writing and composing. Over the course of the next few months they built songs from various bits and pieces and eventually had an entire album ready for the studio.

After pre-production was completed in Los Angeles, everyone regrouped in Rockfield Studios near Monmouth, Wales. This was the same studio where they had recorded the *Dehumanizer* album in 1991.

Recording the album went extremely smooth and only took three weeks. During recording the guys would spend some time at the oft frequented pub talking about what they were gonna call the new album. "We had a couple bottles of really strong cider," said Ronnie, "and we started chucking some ideas about. They were certainly not the titles we were going to use. I think one was *Hemorrhoids*. Another one they came up with was *Preparation H and H.* "Of course," said Ronnie, "they're not going to be used; it was the cider talking. We had lots of laughs."[201]

The laughs didn't end at the pub. As usual there was no shortage of pranks to be played, especially when Vinny was around.

Typically, when Vinny played he would dry his sweat-soaked hair with a blow dryer whenever there was a break. But on one occasion, the dryer quit working. Tony's guitar tech, Mike Clement took a look at it and in no time had the dryer operational and Vinny couldn't be happier. It was then that Tony struck. While Vinny was

---

[201] YouTube video, the making of *The Devil You Know*.

taking a break Tony filled the dryer with talcum powder and he, Ronnie and Geezer waited.

After Vinny returned the guys played some tracks and Vinny worked up a good sweat. As soon as they were finished Vinny pulled out his dryer right on cue and POOF! In an instant he was covered in white powder. Seeing Vinny covered from head to toe had everyone laughing, including Vinny, who was good-natured even when he was the brunt of a joke.

The Devil You Know was released April 28, 2009 and right from the start it was well received. Critics were raving, with some calling it the best metal album of the year while others were praising it as a masterpiece. *Metal Hammer* magazine described the album as "one of the heaviest releases of the year."

Well-known music writer Martin Popoff thought the album was better than *Dehumanizer*, but didn't like it as much as *Mob Rules* or *Heaven and Hell*. He went on to give his thoughts saying, "This is the follow-up to the taster that was three tracks on the greatest hits album, *The Dio Years*. We already got a taste of this music and then when the album came out, *The Devil You Know*, it's basically a single 53-minute album. It's very, very similar to that material which again is very similar to where Dio's head-space had been basically throughout the '90s and the 2000s. He was loving this slow doomy idea, so he was exploring that with Rowan Robertson and all of those records he was doing whether they were concept albums or not—certainly *Magica* was a lot like that. And it was a little bit of a follow-up to what he was doing on *Dehumanizer*, so he almost in a sense is bending Tony's will to his style of Dio music that he had been doing for a long, long time, essentially starting with *Lock up the Wolves* and *Strange Highways.*"

"So almost every song on this record is slow and I'm not crazy about that form of Dio music or Sabbath music; the super slow stuff. But, if anybody can sell it, it's these guys and especially Vinny Appice who does a really good job of playing slow songs. His fills are kept somewhat in check, but he's a guy who is very creative as a drummer and he will do amazing cool fills if given the space and when you have a slow song there is a lot of space to do that. But no, he's very disciplined on this record and they get a great production sound out of Mike Exeter. It's just a very cool, powerful, heavy metal old school sound. It doesn't sound particularly modern, it doesn't sound particularly dated either, it's just a very, very good quality sound."

"Essentially the songs all sound very similar. I suppose a couple of the faster ones are my favorites and that would be "Eating the Cannibals" and "Neverwhere." "Eating the Cannibals" was a fairly popular song. But I guess the most popular songs would have been the opener "Atom and Evil" which, you know, Dio has very clever lyrics on here. They are along the tried and true Sabbath themes but he is very clever with his wordplay, very poetic. "Atom and Evil" is a really cool one and "Bible Black" is a really cool story that was kinda the erstwhile single that was pushed forward. Ronnie's vocals are incredible, you know, great enunciation of all the words; you can understand what he is saying throughout the album and Tony's solos are very cool too. So I guess the one thing I don't like about it; too many slow songs. But I love the chemistry of the band."[202]

Vinny gave his feelings on the album saying, "This record is probably not as dark as *Dehumanizer*. Some of it is and some of it isn't. I would say maybe it's still awfully heavy and it's got a lot of melodic overtones to it. But I think it's a little bit more modern sounding, a little bit more polished and there's some great vocal melodies and some cool riffs."[203]

The album debuted at #8 on the Billboard charts in America and fan response was overwhelmingly positive.

---

[202] Martin Popoff interview with James Curl.
[203] Heaven and Hell, The Devil You Know part 1, YouTube interview 2010.

Most felt it was a great doom metal album and the most inspired work that Ronnie and company had put out in decades.

The album featured a well-crafted collection of heavy metal songs and crushing Iommi riffs. However, for some, the overall slowness of the songs was a bit lumbering. On the up-side there was no denying that Ronnie's vocal performance was outstanding. For all his years, he was now 66, he could still sing with strength and melodic skill that belied his age. And even though his voice had become a little deeper, it had lost none of its raw fierceness and only a little of its falsetto.

With a shiny new album to show off, Heaven & Hell headed over to South America in May of 2009. Two months later they were in Germany at the Wacken open air festival. The show was recorded for the live DVD *Neon Nights: 30 Years of Heaven & Hell,* which was released in 2010 and would turn out to be Ronnie's last filmed show.

A few day later the guys were back in America for the last stretch of their tour. Their 15-show run began in Seattle and ended at the House of Blues in Atlantic City, New Jersey on August 29, 2009. Despite the show being at a small venue the guys had a good time playing and felt it was a fitting way to end the tour. Unknown to everyone at the time, sadly the show would be turn out to be the last one Ronnie would ever play.

Returning to L.A. a few days later Ronnie was surprised to find a couple of Los Angeles police officers waiting for him at the airport, and an urgent message from Wendy saying, "Call me, call me—I'm at the police station." After speaking to Wendy and the officers, Ronnie found out that a man had climbed up a telephone pole and was threatening to commit suicide. He was saying that "the man on the silver mountain told me to jump," and unless he gets to speak to Ronnie Dio he was going to do it.

With no time to waste, the officers rushed Ronnie through with a full police escort to the man's location. Once there the fire department put Ronnie in a cherry picker and sent him up. Face to face with the distraught man, Ronnie talked to him and convinced the fellow to come down. With the man safe, Ronnie returned home.

Never one to pound his chest, the incident went largely unnoticed and was quickly forgotten.

Chapter Fourteen
The Final Curtain

For months during the *The Devil You Know* tour Ronnie had been suffering from persistent and painful stomach problems. Although he suffered quietly, he did mention to Tony a few times that he had a problem with his stomach. He told Tony that he was constantly going to the bathroom and taking antacid.

It wasn't just Ronnie who was having problems on the tour; Vinny and Tony had issues as well. "On the first leg of our North American tour in 2009," said Geezer, "Tony Iommi's hand ligaments were in a bad way, Vinny Appice's shoulder became dislocated and Ronnie was having terrible stomach pains. We decided to cut the tour, get healthy and carry on the following year."

Concerned with Ronnie's health, Tony asked on more than one occasion if he would like to go and get it checked out. Ronnie's response was that when the tour was over he would see a doctor and sort himself out.

Though not feeling well during the tour, Ronnie fought through it and performed as usual.

"On some nights," said Tony, "he was in agony on stage but he'd just carry on. Sometimes he was on his last leg but he insisted on completing each and every show for the tour. He was the ultimate professional. For Ronnie the show must go on. He didn't want to disappoint the fans."[204]

After returning home in August, Ronnie planned on doing a short Dio tour. He gathered up Scott, Simon, and Rudy and then got back in touch with Doug, who agreed to take up the guitar reins once again. The band started rehearsals but Ronnie's stomach problems continued to

---

[204] Black Sabbath star Tony Iommi says no more Heaven and Hell gigs after death of Ronnie James Dio, the *Sunday Mercury*, July 13, 2010.

worsen. By late October he could no longer ignore it. A few days later Ronnie went to see his doctor. Following a series of tests it was found that Ronnie had stage four stomach cancer as well as a bleeding ulcer and a tumor in his stomach. Treatment was scheduled to start immediately.

A few weeks later on November 26, 2009, Wendy released an official statement saying, "Ronnie has been diagnosed with the early stages of stomach cancer. We are starting treatment immediately at the Mayo Clinic. After he kills this dragon, Ronnie will be back on stage, where he belongs, doing what he loves best, performing for his fans. Long live rock 'n' roll, long live Ronnie James Dio."

Following the diagnosis any thoughts of a tour were quickly quashed and Ronnie began flying out to MD Anderson Cancer Center in Houston, Texas every two weeks for chemotherapy treatment. The trips were exhausting and took a toll on the weakened singer. Ronnie, however, took it in stride and although the diagnosis was grave, he was positive and upbeat. To help Ronnie through his difficult ordeal Geezer would often accompany him on his trips to Houston. Speaking of Geezer and his incredible friendship, Ronnie said, "He said 'I want to go through what Ronnie is going through. I want to be here for him.'"[205]

While in the hospital for a treatment session, Ronnie was interviewed, saying "I'm lucky that I am a very hard person, and strong within my beliefs, so this hasn't really been a problem for me. I just look at cancer, 'I'll kick the hell out of you.'" Ronnie then went on to say, "I refuse to be beaten in any way, shape or form, so I'm gonna beat this too."[206]

Word of Ronnie's cancer quickly spread throughout the rock 'n' roll community and friends and fans were

---

[205] Channel 39 News, YouTube video.
[206] Ibid.

shocked and saddened. Hearing the terrible news, Rowan Robertson said, "All I remember thinking was hoping for the best and that he would get better."

After several weeks of treatment, Ronnie began to show signs of improvement and the doctors found that the tumor in his stomach had started to shrink.

Excited with the positive news Wendy released a statement in March of 2010 saying, "It has been Ronnie's seventh chemo, another cat scan and another endoscopy, and the results are good—the main tumor has shrunk considerably, and our visits to Houston (cancer clinic in Texas) are now every three weeks instead of every two weeks."[207]

Having noticed that Ronnie had been keeping a low profile since his diagnosis, fans were hopeful and optimistic when Ronnie made an appearance at the *Revolver* Golden Gods Awards on April 8th. Ronnie had been honored with the award for Best Metal Singer for his work on *The Devil You Know* album and he wanted to be there in person to accept it. Winning the award made him the oldest recipient at age 67.

Coming out on stage Ronnie was all smiles as the crowd chanted "Dio! Dio! Dio!" and he flashed his legendary devil horns.

Accepting the award Ronnie said, "I want to thank you so very, very much, what a cool award. It's great to be back amongst people again, especially since it's been a little while since I've been able to do that. But I feel pretty good and can't wait to get back on the stage again." Despite Ronnie's optimism, the award show would be his final public appearance.

After his attendance at the award show Ronnie and his band mates were enthusiastic. They began talking about doing a tour of Europe starting in June and going through August of 2010.

---

[207] UltimateGuitar, Ronnie James Dio Wining Cancer Battle, March 17, 2010.

"The tumor had been shrinking and they gave him the go-ahead to come back out on the road," said Tony. "Our summer tour got the green light and we were constantly on the phone talking about what songs we'd do. Ronnie was really excited. We were going to try out some new songs, the band was really tight, we were on fire. He was so looking forward to the European tour. It was going to be a new lease on life. But early in May they found that the cancer had spread to Ronnie's liver, and things went downhill pretty quickly. We cancelled all the tour dates, still hoping against hope that he'd pull through. He was a fighter, after all."[208]

From there Ronnie's health deteriorated at a rapid pace. Geezer Butler who was there for Ronnie's last few days, recalls the time, saying, "On Friday, Wendy called to say she had taken Ronnie to the hospital. The pain had become unbearable. We got to the hospital around 2:00 p.m. The doctor eventually sedated him. More and more friends were coming to visit; we took it in turns to hold Ronnie's hand and whisper our thoughts to him. Wendy wouldn't leave his side—she stayed curled up on his bed the whole night. Gloria's assistant, Debi, kept her company. I emailed Tony to prepare him for bad news."

By Saturday a number of friends had shown up and things had gotten worse. "There was no mistaking Ronnie's room," said Geezer. "There were around 25 to 30 friends outside his room. We knew the end was imminent. We all wanted to say our goodbyes. It was a day filled with tears and reflection. In the evening, the chaplain came and we all gathered around Ronnie's bed and prayed. Ronnie wasn't going easily. At 11 p.m., most of us left, leaving Wendy her privacy to say her last farewell. The devastation was palpable."

By early Sunday morning the news came. "7:46 a.m. As we were preparing to leave for the hospital," said

---

[208] Black Sabbath star Tony Iommi says no more Heaven and Hell gigs after death of Ronnie James Dio, the *Sunday Mercury*, July 13, 2010.

Geezer, "Gloria called Wendy to see if she wanted a coffee or any breakfast—she broke the sad news. Ronnie had just passed away."

Claude Schnell, who was celebrating his birthday on Saturday, recalls the last moments he spent with his friend. "By Saturday there were rumors online that Ronnie was already dead. After the birthday party Sheila and I headed over to the hospital to see Ronnie. It was probably three in the morning which of course was after visiting hours. So, I put on my New York hat and said, 'Look, my friend is here and he is dying and I need to see him.'

'Who's your friend?' asked the nurse.

"So I gave them the name and they said, 'Oh, yes please come in.'"

"So they gave us special passes and we were allowed to roam the hospital and we found the room. Ronnie was on a morphine drip and Wendy was curled up on the bed next to him asleep. Ronnie's assistant Steve Mignardi knew who I was so he let me stay for a while."

"As soon as I walked in I sensed that he knew I was there. So I carefully went to the far side of the bed and his hands were folded on his chest and I put my hand on his hand. They weren't cold but they weren't animated either. I thought I felt him react to my hand being there. And I said a silent prayer and I squeezed his hand and I walked away."

"So off we go, got home and it's like 5:30 and about 6:00 by the time I'm ready to lay down. And as I get ready to lay my head on the pillow I remember thinking *'He's gone.'* And sure enough, I wake up to a message on my answering machine that he had passed."[209]

Geezer Butler praised Wendy, saying, "Wendy Dio has been a true saint through all this. She has been with Ronnie every step of the way. Her courage has amazed

---

[209] Claude Schnell interview with James Curl.

us all. Even as I write, she is ensuring that Ronnie has the finest send-off possible. God bless you, Wendy."

Jeff Pilson recalled Wendy's loyalty to Ronnie as well, saying, "You could never underestimate how close their bond was, no matter what was going on with the outer surface of their relationship. They had something very deep; you know they never divorced for a reason, because they had something that was very, very strong. I think it kinda defied traditional definitions, but whatever it was, it was very strong. Wendy was so amazing during the time of his passing. She was unbelievably dedicated. She literally devoted every ounce of energy at the end which is what he needed and what she felt she needed to do. It just kinda exemplified how strong their bond was."[210]

Following Ronnie's passing on May 16th Wendy released a short statement. "Today my heart is broken. Ronnie passed away at 7:45 a.m. Many, many friends and family were able to say their private goodbyes before he peacefully passed away. Ronnie knew how much he was loved by all. We so appreciate the love and support that you have all given us. Please give us a few days of privacy to deal with this terrible loss. Please know he loved you all and his music will live on forever."

Ronnie's funeral was held on May 29th while his memorial service took place the following day at Forest Lawn Memorial Park in the Hollywood Hills. The service was hosted by Ronnie's friend Eddie Trunk of That Metal Show. Throughout the day nearly 2,000 fans came to pay their respects to the iconic singer. With the grounds filled to capacity, fans that couldn't make it inside gathered in large numbers outside and watched the proceedings on monitors.

Longtime Dio keyboardist Scott Warren began the memorial service with an arrangement of Dio's "This Is

---

[210] Jeff Pilson interview with James Curl.

Your Life" on piano. Geoff Tate delivered a touching rendition of Leonard Cohen's "Hallelujah," and Paul Shortino choked back tears while singing the Beatles' "In My Life."

Other performances included singer John Payne of the band Asia, and Anthrax front man Joey Belladonna, who performed "Man on the Silver Mountain."

The highlight of the musical performances came from Ronnie's longtime friend Glenn Hughes, who was Ronnie's favorite singer. Glenn crooned, "Coast to Coast" as well as "Catch the Rainbow." Both songs received standing ovations.

Several of Ronnie's close friends and family members, including longtime friend and assistant Willie Fyfe and Dave Feinstein, took to the podium between song sets.

"He touched all of us with his music and his message and his magic," said Dave. "I know that Ronnie truly loved all of you. He had a great appreciation for your loyalty. I'm talking about all you out there, all the fans. His fans and followers were one of the most important things in the world to him. And he really cared about all of you out there that have been to shows and would watch Ronnie stand outside the bus for hours signing autographs until the very last one was done, he really cared about the fans and he really appreciated everything the fans did for him. So even though we can't see him anymore or touch him anymore and he's not physically here, his vision will remain in our hearts and our minds and he will continue to inspire us, whether you're a musician or you're someone that's a fan and appreciates what he's done."[211]

Ronnie's son Dan spoke of his father, giving heartfelt reflections on some of his memories, while also issuing a stern warning to "get screened regularly and to treat our

---

[211] Ronnie James Dio remembered in L.A, the Associated Press, May 31, 2010.

bodies properly. I beg you not to make the mistake my father made; for dad the show always had to go on. He ignored the warning signs for years and all along the cancer was growing and mutating from something which was probably easily defeatable into a monster which even Dio couldn't slay."

Following Ronnie's funeral, things gradually returned to normal for family members, friends and fans. Over the subsequent years Ronnie's memory has remained strong and he has been heaped with accolades.

In his hometown of Cortland, Ronnie was honored by having a street named after him called Dio Way. On July 10, 2011, Cortland held an all-day event showcasing several local bands for a benefit for the Stand Up and Shout Cancer Fund, a charity started by Wendy after Ronnie's passing. Moreover, part of the proceeds from the event went to fund a memorial music scholarship for the local city high school. In addition, Wendy has since started the Bowl for Ronnie, an annual event that raises money for the Stand Up and Shout Cancer Fund.

In October of 2010 a statue was unveiled in the coastal town of Kavarna in Bulgaria. The decision to erect the monument was taken up by the municipal administration, with the most active supporter being Kavarna's Mayor Tzonko Tzonev, who is a huge metal fan.

Other supporters included leading musicians, singers and journalists. Dio was one of the very first heavy metal icons to play in Kavarna. In fact, Ronnie performed in Bulgaria five times and took an active part in the campaign for liberating the Bulgarian nurses held in prison in Libya for eight years. Sculptors Alexander Petrov and Krasimir Krastev-Lomsky spent two months working on the statue, which is approximately six-and-a-half feet tall and is combined with large stones taken from the sea. The statue, which was funded entirely through donations, was placed in the city's central park, as part of the soon to be built "Alley of Rock."

Two months after the unveiling of the statue, Ronnie's father Pat passed away on December 28th at the age of 92. He was laid to rest next to Anna in St. Mary's Cemetery in Cortland.

On January 18, 2017, at the newly opened Hall of Heavy Metal History, Ronnie was the first recipient to be inducted along with Rudy Sarzo, Frankie Banali, Lemmy Kilmister, Ross 'The Boss' Friedman, Vinny Appice, Don Airey, Andy Zildjian and Randy Rhoads.

His enshrinement was well deserved and something that has been shamefully overlooked by the Rock and Roll Hall of Fame for far too long.

Accolades, however, are not something Ronnie ever needed. His musical legacy as well as his character and morality speak for themselves. One needs to look no further than the work Ronnie did with charities like Hear 'n Aid and Children of the Night to know that cared deeply about people. His work with these organizations is something that he should be remembered for as well as his music.

Thankfully, the gift of his music and that unmistakable voice, that touched so many lives, will live on forever. And though some may lament the loss of Ronnie, all they have to do is play one of his songs to know that his spirit will never truly be gone as long as there is music. Even now Ronnie's music is being discovered and embraced by new generations and enjoyed by those who grew up with him. And that is something that would have made Ronnie happy, because Ronnie was always about making the fans happy.

Eulogy

By Claude Schnell

"With the dawn of the new day on May 16, 2010 came the end of an era. When Ronnie left us in the early hours of that morning, he took with him a presence that will never be replaced. But in the wake of this tragedy, when the fog of overwhelming sadness slowly began to lift and give way to the first glimpses of lucidity, it became clear that the gifts this giant of a man had left behind were enough to fill several lifetimes. This was a man who pursued, and I might add achieved, excellence in every arena he traversed. This was never more apparent than when he would sing. And sing he did, with his voice propelling each and every note he ever sang to the zenith of vocal performance. His voice was the stuff of legend, as were his skills as a writer, a musician, and a producer. But he was also a man of intensity, character, and wisdom. A man whose generosity of spirit knew no limits. And this was never more apparent than in his relationships. Anyone who had the good fortune to know Ronnie knows this to be true."

"I, for one, know this to be true. Having played with Ronnie has left me with memories and lessons that will last a lifetime. For that, I am and always will be grateful. But I am truly humbled by the knowledge that Ronnie counted me amongst his friends. The imprint of that friendship will continue to affect me every single day, for the rest of my life."

"Farewell, my friend, you will be missed in more ways than you know."

An older Ronnie. Photo courtesy Joey Belfiore.

Fan artwork on display at Ronnie's funeral. Photo courtesy of Mike Jones.

Photo courtesy of Mike Jones.

Ronnie's casket. Photo courtesy of Mike Jones.

Photo courtesy of Mike Jones.

Dio Way in Cortland, New York.
Photo courtesy of Mike Donohue.

Ronnie's statue in Kavarna, Bulgaria.

Discography

Ronnie and the Red Caps

Singles

Year	A-Side	B-Side	Format
1958	Conquest	Lover	7"
1958	Judy I Love You	-	7"
1960	An Angel Is Missing	What I'd Say	7"

Ronnie did not sing lead vocals on "Conquest" or "Judy I Love You"

Ronnie Dio and the Prophets

Singles

Year	A-Side	B-Side	Format	Label
1962	The Ooh-Poo-Pah-Doo	Love Pains	7"	Atlantic
1962	Will You Still Love Me Tomorrow	Bad Man In Town	7"	Audiodisc/Swan
1963	Gonna Make It Alone	Swingin' Street	7"	Lawn
1963	Mr. Misery	Our Year	7"	Swan
1963	Che Tristezza Senza Te	Our Year	7"	Derby

Year	A-side	B-side	Format	Label
1964	Mr. Misery (Mr. Misery)	Our Year	7"	Stateside
1964	Love Potion No. 9	Love Potion No. 9	7"	Valex
1965	Say You're Mine Again	Where You Gonna Run To Girl	7"	Kapp
1965	Smiling By Day (Crying By Night)	Dear Darling (I Won't Be Comin' Home)	7"	Kapp
1965	Walking Alone	The Way Of Love	7"	Kapp
1967	Walking In Different Circles	10 Days With Brenda	7"	Parkway

Albums

1963 Dio at Dominos, LP

The album sleeve notes this is a "live" recording, but it is not live in the sense of being recorded at a concert. Most likely, the album was cut live in the studio.

The Electric Elves

Year	A-Side	B-Side	Format
1967	Hey, Look Me Over	It Pays To Advertise	7"

The Elves

Year	A-Side	B-Side	Format	Label
1969	Walking In Different Circles	She's Not The Same	7"	Decca
1970	Amber Velvet	West Virginia	7"	MCA
1970	Amber Velvet	West Virginia	7"	Decca

Bootlegs

Year	Title	Format	Label	Cat. No.	Country	Notes
1971	Live At The Beacon	LP	-	-	USA	Bootleg

Elf

Studio Albums

Year	Title	Format	Label	Notes
1972	*Elf*	LP, CS, CD	Epic	-
1974	*Carolina County Ball*	LP, CS, CD	Purple, Line, Safari, MGM	Known as *L.A. 59* in USA

225

Year	Title	Format	Label
1975	Trying to Burn the Sun	LP, CS	Safari, Interfusion	-

Compilations

Year	Title	Format	Label
1974	The History of Syracuse Music, Vol. VI	LP	ECEIP
1978	The Gargantuan Elf Album	CD	Safari
1989	20 Years of Syracuse Rock	CS	-
1994	The Elf Albums	CD	Connoisseur Collection, Festival

Bootlegs

Year	Title	Format
1972	Live At The Bank	LP
1973	Live! And My Soul Shall Be Lifted	LP, CD

Rainbow

- *Ritchie Blackmore's Rainbow* (1975) **UK Silver**
- *Rising* (1976) **UK Gold**
- *On Stage* (1977) **UK Silver**
- *Long Live Rock 'n' Roll* (1978) **UK Silver**
- *Finyl Vinyl* (1986)
- *Live in Germany 1976* (1990)

- *Ritchie Blackmore: Rock Profile Volume Two* (1991)
- *Live In Munich 1977* (2006)
- *Deutschland Tournee 1976* (2006)
- *Live In Cologne* (2007)
- *Live In Düsseldorf* (2007)
- *Live In Nurnberg* (2007)
- *The Polydor Years: 1975-1986* (2007)

Black Sabbath

Heaven and Hell (1980) **US Platinum UK Gold**
Black And Blue (VHS) (1980)
- *Heavy Metal: Music from the Motion Picture* (1981) (One track, an alternate take of "The Mob Rules")
- *Mob Rules* (1981) **US Gold UK Silver**
- *Live Evil* (1982)
- *Dehumanizer* (1992)
- *Black Sabbath: The Dio Years* (2007)
- *Live at Hammersmith Odeon* (2007)
- *The Rules of Hell* (Boxed Set) (2008)

Dio

- *Holy Diver* (1983) **US Platinum UK Silver**
- *The Last in Line* (1984) **US Platinum UK Silver**
- *Sacred Heart* (1985) **US Gold**

- *Intermission* (1986)
- *Dream Evil* (1987)
- *Lock up the Wolves* (1990)
- *Dio - Sacred Heart: The DVD (1991)*
- *Diamonds – The Best of Dio*
- *Strange Highways* (1993)
- *Angry Machines* (1996)
- *Inferno - Last in Live* (1998)
- *Magica* (2000)
- *The Very Beast of Dio* (2000) **US Gold**
- *Killing the Dragon* (2002)
- *Master of the Moon* (2004)
- *We Rock ~ Dio (DVD 2005)*
- *Evil or Divine - Live In New York City* (2005)
- *Holy Diver - Live* (2006)
- *The Very Beast of Dio Vol. 2* (2012) - (Posthumous)

Heaven & Hell

- *Live from Radio City Music Hall* (2007) **US Gold**
- *The Devil You Know* (2009)
- *Neon Nights: 30 Years of Heaven & Hell* (2010)

Guest appearances

- Bobby Comstock & The Counts: "Your Big Brown Eyes" 7" Single (1960), "Run My Heart" 7" Single (1963)
- The Angels: *My Boyfriend's Back* 7" Single (1963), My Boyfriend's Back (1963)
- Austin Gravelding: *Self Made Man* (1970)
- Roger Glover: *The Butterfly Ball and the Grasshopper's Feast* (1974)
- David Coverdale: *Northwinds* (1978)

- Kerry Livgren: *Seeds of Change* (1980), *The Best of Kerry Livgren* (2002)
- Heaven: *Where Angels Fear to Tread* (1983)
- Rough Cutt: *LA's Hottest Unsigned Rock Bands* (1983), *KLOS 95 1/2 Rock To Riches* (1983), *Rough Cutt* (1984), *Rough Cutt Live* (1996), *Anthology* (2008)
- Hellion: *12 Commandments In Metal* (1985), *To Hellion And Back* (2014) *(production only)*
- Hear 'n Aid: *Hear 'n Aid* (1986), "Stars" 7"/12" Single (1986), *Hear 'n Aid: The Sessions* (VHS video) (1986)
- Eddie Hardin & Guests: *Wizard's Convention* (1994)
- Dog Eat Dog: *Play Games* (1996)
- Munetaka Higuchi With Dream Castle: *Free World* (1997)
- Pat Boone: *In a Metal Mood: No More Mr. Nice Guy* (1997)
- Various Artists: *Humanary Stew: A tribute to Alice Cooper* (1999), *Not The Same Old Song And Dance: A Tribute to Aerosmith* (1999), *We Wish you a Metal Xmas and a Headbanging New Year* (2008)
- Deep Purple: *In Concert with The London Symphony Orchestra* (1999), *Live at the Rotterdam Ahoy* (2001), *The Soundboard Series* (2001)
- Eddie Ojeda: *Axes 2 Axes* (2005)
- Ian Gillan: *Gillan's Inn* (2006)
- Queensrÿche: *Operation: Mindcrime II* (2006), *Mindcrime at the Moore* (2007)
- Tenacious D: *The Pick of Destiny* (2006)
- Girlschool: *Legacy* (2008)

- David "Rock" Feinstein: *Bitten By The Beast* (2010)
- The Rods: Vengeance (2011)

Other media

- *The Black Sabbath Story* (Documentary, vol. 2) (1992)
- *Metal: A Headbanger's Journey* (Documentary) (2005)
- *Heavy: The Story of Heavy Metal* (Documentary) (2006)
- *Tenacious D in the Pick of Destiny* (Film) (2006)
- *That Metal Show* - Season 2, Episode 8: *Heaven & Hell* (2009)

Index

Accept, band 96
Aerosmith 82
Airey, Don 216
Alford, Dave 77
Aldrich, Doug 183, 184, 192, 2008
Aldridge, Tommy
Alice in Chains 156, 159
Angry Machines, album 170, 175
Appice, Carmine 62
Appice, Vinny 61-72, 74, 95, 98, 101, 103, 142, 143, 148, 149, 154, 155, 158-163, 167, 168, 173, 177, 198, 199 201, 203-205, 208, 216,
Arcuri, Angelo 74, 92, 95, 144
Arden, Don 55, 57
Arden, Sharon (Osbourne) 55

Babs, Lil 16
Bach, Johann Sebastian 41
Bad Finger 32
Bain, Jimmy 44, 47, 48, 69-74, 81, 84, 85, 88-91, 95, 98, 99, 100, 103, 147, 149, 151, 152, 154, 155, 161, 163, 167, 177, 191, 192
Banali, Frankie, 95, 216
Barry, Chuck 11, 71
Barrett, Randy 75
Beach Boys 83
Beck, Jeff 41, 44
Belfiore, Joey 92, 93, 94, 95, 188
Belladonna, Joey 214
Berardi, Loretta 17, 25, 26
Best, Jerry 173
Birch, Martin 41, 48
Bitten by the Beast, album, 201
Black, Jack 181, 182, 194, 195
Black Rain, band 184
Blackmore, Babs 42

Blackmore, Ritchie 34, 35, 38-53, 161, 172, 175, 197
Black Sabbath 21, 54, 55, 57, 58, 60, 61, 62, 63, 67, 68, 72, 82, 98, 156, 157, 159, 160, 161, 175, 177, 195, 200
Blanc, Mel 165
Bloom, Eric 94
Bottoff, Dick 14, 15, 16, 17, 18, 19, 23
Bonham, Jason 171
Breme, Simon 16
Brian's Idols 18, 20, 29
Brown, Mick 1, 95
Butler, Geezer, 54, 55, 56, 58, 62, 64-68, 156, 159, 198, 199, 201, 208, 209, 211, 212
Byrds, the 21

Cactus 32
Campbell, Vivian 70-75, 81, 83, 84, 85, 87-91, 95, 97-100 138, 139, 143, 145, 161, 175
Canedy, Carl 200, 201
Carey, Tony 45, 48, 49, 50
Carolina Country Ball, album 37, 38
Carter, Goree 11
Cavazo, Carlos 95
Cinders, 9
Clark, Mark 48, 50
Clement, Mike 203
Columbia's 30th Street studio 25
Comstock, Bobby 12, 16
Consroe, Pauli 16
Cook, Teddy 154
Cooper, Alice 32, 202
Coverdale, David 151
Cristofanilli, Joey 77, 78, 84
Cristofanilli, Mary 84
Crosby, Robbin 92

D'Addario, Raymond 51
Daisley, Bob 50, 51, 52, 173
Davis, Clive 34
De Carlo, Lee 66, 67
De Carlo, Yvonne 66
Dehumanizer, album 158, 159, 175, 203, 204
DeMartini, Warren, 92
Deep Purple, 21, 34, 35, 36, 38-42, 51, 55
Def Leppard 70, 104
Dennison, Larry 173
Derakh, Amir, 95
Derringer, Rick 62
Devil You Know, album 204, 210
De Wolf, Billy 13, 14,
Dharma, buck 95
Dickinson, Bruce 171, 188
Dioguardi, Johnny 15
Dio at Dominos, album 16
Dokken 77
Dokken, Don 94, 167, 168
Donohue, Mike 29
Doors, the 21
Dream Evil, album 143, 144, 145
Driscoll, Gary 19, 20, 22, 23, 24, 28, 30, 38, 40, 44
Dr. X 196, 197
DuBrow, Kevin 94
Dunn, Sam 188
Dysfunctional album 168, 199

Edwards, Steve 37, 40
Electric Elves, the 21, 22, 31
Elton, John 48, 181
Elf 21, 26, 29, 32, 34, 35, 36, 38, 39, 41, 43, 44, 58, 200
Elf, album 35
Elves, the 25, 26, 27, 28, 29, 30, 31, 32
Exeter, Mike 205

Feinstein, Dave 17, 19-26, 28, 29, 30, 36, 37, 200, 214
Fleetwood Mack 41
Freeman, Andrew 103
Free Will, band 29
Freidman, Ross 216
Fulton, Clay 17
Fyfe, Willie 214

Gass, Kyle 182, 194
Gaxiola, Wendy (Dio) 42, 48, 49-53, 72, 76, 78, 87-90, 92, 98, 100, 103, 139, 150, 152, 154, 157, 163, 164, 173, 187, 199, 206, 209, 211, 212, 213
Gibb, Barry 58
Gillis, Brad 94
Ginocchio, Bob 80
Glover, Roger 34, 35, 44
Goldy, Craig 95, 98, 102, 138, 142-147, 161, 174, 175, 177, 178, 183, 192
Great White 77
Grijalva, Tracy 161-169, 173, 174, 175, 180
Gruber, Craig 37, 38, 40, 43, 44, 58

Hagar, Chris 95
Haley, Bill 11
Halford, Rob 47, 94
Harlot, band 44
Hart, Colin 36, 41, 43, 47, 48, 49, 51
Hear 'N Aid 88-96
Heaven and Hell, album 58, 59, 64, 73, 204
Heaven & Hell, band 140, 200, 202, 206
Hendrix, Jimmy 21, 96
Hoey, Gary 148, 153
Holly, Buddy 11
Holmes, Chris 95
Holy Diver, album, 74, 75, 76, 81, 82, 83, 85, 86, 92, 98, 100, 104, 168, 174-177, 189
Hughes, Glenn 79, 92, 165, 214
Ian Gillan, band 44

Iommi, Tony 54-57, 59, 61, 62-68, 157-161, 182, 188, 197-201, 203, 204, 206, 208
Iron Maiden 37, 70

Jackson, Michael 83, 88
Jason Bonham, band 171
J. Geils Band 38
Johansson, Jens 155
John Elton 83
Jo Jo Gunne 32
Judas Priest 37, 47

Karloff, Boris 55
Killing The Dragon, album 183, 187, 193
Kilmister, Lemmy 188, 216
Kiss 96, 184
Kottack, James 173

L.A./59 37
Last in Line, album 85, 86, 98, 168
Lanza, Mario 8
Lawless, Blackie 95
Led Zeppelin, 21, 27, 28, 55
Lee, Jake E. 69, 77, 78, 92, 138
Lee, Louis, Dr. 178
Lennon, John 64
Lion, band 184
Lock up the Wolves, album 152, 153, 159, 204
Logan, Oni 157
Long Live Rock 'n' Roll, album 48, 51, 52
Lynch, George 95

Magic 77
Magica, album 175-180, 183, 204
191, 192, 193
Malmsteen, Yngwie 95, 161
Manning, Sean 148
Mars, Mick 95

Marx, Richard 178
Martin, Tony 157
Master of the Moon, album 191, 193, 197
McKean, Michael 91
Megadeth, band 147
Meniketti, Dave 94
Metallica 37, 156
Mickey Rat 38
Mignardi, Steve 212
Miller, Ralph 7
Mob Rules, album 64, 73, 199, 204
Modine, Matthew 96
Morand, Larry 152
Motörhead 69, 70, 96
Moore, Gary 74
Moore, Vinny 161
Motley Crue 26, 77, 148
Murray, Dave 95
Musci, Jack 12, 14,

Neil, Vince 95
Nicholls, Geoff 57, 58
Nirvana 156
Nugent, Ted 95

Operation: Mindcrime II, album 196, 197
Osbourne, Ozzy 54-59, 150, 160, 178, 181, 194, 200
Ojeda, Eddie 95

Pilson, Jeff 1, 2, 3, 161, 164, 167-170, 171, 173, 192, 193, 194
Padavona, Anna, 6, 197
Padavona, Anthony, 7
Padavona, Bill 60,
Padavona, Danny 25, 26, 51, 214
Padavona, Erminia 7, 59, 60
Padavona, Patrick 6, 12, 215
Paice, Ian 34, 35

Pantas, Jimmy 13
Pantas, Nicky 7, 12, 14, 16-25, 92
Pantera 159
Payne, Bruce 36, 47
Payne, John 214
Pearl Jam 155
Perry, Joe 82
Pick of Destiny, the 194, 196
Pitney, Gene 20
Poison 77
Popoff, Martin 76, 185, 204
Powell, Cozy 44, 45, 48, 51, 52, 157, 158
Presley, Elvis 11

Quartz 57
Quatermass, band 39
Queensrÿche 82, 196, 202
Quiet Riot 77, 194

Rage Against The Machine 159
Rainbow 40-53, 58, 157, 172, 176
Rainbow club 39, 42, 45, 47, 48, 82, 152
Rainbow Rising, album 45, 47, 58
Ratt 77, 78
Rhoads, Randy 92, 216
Ritchie Blackmore's Rainbow, album 41, 58
Robertson, John 152
Robertson, Rowan 148, 150, 151, 152, 153, 154, 156, 157, 161, 204, 210
Rods, the 36, 200, 201
Rogers, Tommy 10, 12, 16, 18, 19
Ronnie Dio and the Prophets 15, 16, 18-22, 31
Ronnie and the Rumblers, 12
Ronnie and the Red Caps 12, 13, 15, 31
Roscoe, William 38
Roth, David Lee 92
Rough Cutt 69, 81, 98, 138, 139, 140

Sarzo, Rudy 95, 194, 208, 216
Sacred Heart, album 87-89, 94, 96, 97, 98, 145, 163
Savatage 147
Saxon 70
Schenker, Michael 161
Sheehan, Billy 92
Schnell, Claude 76-80, 83, 91, 92, 95, 101, 103, 141, 143-149, 153, 154, 212
Schnell, Sheila 145, 148, 212
Schon, Neal 95, 161
Scorpions 84, 96, 171, 173
Shortino, Paul 77, 94, 214
Shearer, Harry 91
Shelton, Jack 19
Simons, Gene 184
Sixx, Nikki 148
Soule, Mickey lee 15, 16, 23-25, 28, 30-35, 37, 38, 40
Soundgarden 156
Strange Highways, album 168, 169, 170, 175, 193, 204
Spears, Britney 60
Spinal Tap, band 91, 142
Smalls, Derek 91
Smith, Adrian 95
Star, Ringo 63
Stein, Mark 95
Stewart, Rod 62, 78, 180
St. Hubbins, David 91
Stone, David 50, 52, 54
Stone Temple pilots 156, 159
Sweet Savage 41, 43, 70, 74
Sykes, John 70

Tate, Geoff 94, 196, 213
Tenacious D. 181, 183, 194
Thaler, Doug 17-23, 25, 26, 30, 31
Thorr, Matt 95
Tolkien, J.R.R 75
Tomes, Sandy 83

Trunk, Eddie 213
Tyler, Steven 82

Vanilla Fudge 62
Vegas Kings, the 12, 13
Vengeance, album 201
Violet's Demise 157

Walsh, Joe 83
Walter, Scott 9
Ward, Bill 54, 56, 57, 61, 62, 198, 199
Warren, Scott 162, 177, 192, 208, 213
W.A.S.P. 77
West, Chas 171
Whitesnake 104, 194
Who, the 27
Wild Horses, band 70, 71
Winter, Edgar 32
Wood, Gary, 8
Wool, Ed 30
Wright, Simon 155, 157, 173, 177, 188, 192, 208

Y&T, band 96

Zappa, Frank 83
Zildjian Andy 216
ZZ Top 36

www.ingramcontent.com/pod-product-compliance
Lightning Source LLC
Chambersburg PA
CBHW071905290426
44110CB00013B/1289